# THE WORSHIP SONGBOOK

**VOLUME
02**

**SONG TITLES
L–Z**

SOVEREIGN GRACE®
MINISTRIES

# COPYRIGHT

This songbook is available through your favorite music retailer or directly from Sovereign Grace Ministries at www.SovereignGraceStore.com

Transcriptions — Roger Hooper and Donald Thomson
Senior Editors — Bob Kauflin and Bo Lotinsky
Proofreaders — Nancy Lotinsky and Tawn O'Connor
Production Coordinator — Rocio Borda
Design — Matthew Wahl and Jeff Martin
Editorial Design — Kevin Meath

SOVEREIGN GRACE®
MINISTRIES

**IMPORTANT INFORMATION REGARDING THE CONGREGATIONAL USE OF THE SONGS IN THIS SONGBOOK**

The **words** of the songs in this publication are covered by a **Church Copyright License** which is available from Christian Copyright Licensing International (CCLI). This allows local-church reproduction and use on Power Point slides or overhead-projector acetates, in service bulletins, song sheets, audio/visual recording, and other formats.

CCLI PROVIDES THE ANSWERS TO YOUR COPYRIGHT QUESTIONS

Full details can be obtained from the CCLI Web site (www.ccli.com) or from the following offices:

Christian Copyright Licensing International (USA)
17201 NE Sacramento Street, Portland, OR 97230, USA
503.257.2230   800.234.2446
Fax: 503.257.2244   executive@ccli.com

Christian Copyright Licensing Ltd. (Europe)
P.O. Box 1339, Eastbourne, East Sussex, BN21 1AD, UK
01323.417711   Fax: 01323.417722   executive@ccli.co.uk

Christian Copyright Licensing Asia-Pacific Pty. Ltd. (Australia)
P.O. Box 6644, Baulkham Hills Business Centre, NSW 2153, Australia
02 9894.5386   800.635.474
Fax: 02 9894.5701   Toll Free Fax: 800.244.477
executive@ccli.com.au

Christian Copyright Licensing Asia-Pacific Pty. Ltd. (New Zealand)
P.O. Box 87-458, Meadowbank, Auckland, New Zealand
09 522.4494   800.373.773
Fax: 09 522.4492   Toll Free Fax: 800.373.773
executive@ccli.com.au

Please note, all texts and music in this book are protected by copyright. If you do not possess a license from CCLI they may **not** be reproduced in any way for sale or private use without the consent of the copyright owner. To obtain copy permission for songs owned or administered by Sovereign Grace Music, please submit your request through one of our music administrators listed below.

Sovereign Grace Ministries Music catalogs (Sovereign Grace Worship and Sovereign Grace Praise) are administered in North America by Integrity Music, 1000 Cody Road, Mobile, AL 36695 (www.integritymusic.com) and the rest of the world by CopyCare International Ltd, P.O. Box 77, Hailsham, E.Sussex, BN27 3EF UK
+44 1323.840942   Fax: +44 1323.849355   sandra@copycare.com

# SONGS

# Let All That Is Within Me
## *I love you, Lord*

Words and Music: Mark Altrogge

Ps 33:1-3, Ps 92:1
Ps 103:1, Ps 147:1
Isa 40:28

# Let Me Count the Ways

## *How do you love me?*

Ps 63:3, Ro 8:28-30
Eph 3:14-19

Words and Music: Mark Altrogge

it- self.    And, Je-sus, your love    is    bet-

-ter    than a - ny- thing else.    You cre-

a - ted    me    to en- joy    you    for- ev- er,    for-

ev - er de- clar - ing    your praise.    Oh, how you love    me,

count- less    are    the    ways.

2. How do you love me? Let me count the ways,
   working all for good mercies ev'ry day.
   How do you love me? I can see your hand
   forming Christ in me by your gracious plan,
   how you love me, how you love me.

# Let Praise Ascend

Mal 1:11, 1Ti 2:8
Rev 5:9-12

Words and Music: Mark Altrogge

# Let the Name of Jesus

Eph 1:7-10, Col 1:16-18
Heb 2:5-9

Words and Music: Mark Altrogge

# Let Us Draw Near

Ro 5:9, 2Co 5:17
Eph 2:4-7, Heb 4:14-16
Heb 12:22-24

Words and Music: Mark Altrogge

# Let Your Joy Come Down

*There is joy in heaven*

Lk 15:10, Rev 5:11-14
Rev 7:13-17

Words and Music: Mark Altrogge

1. There is joy in heav-en, un-ceas-ing joy in your pres-

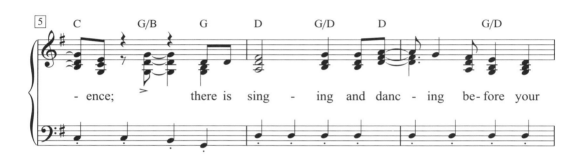

-ence; there is sing-ing and danc-ing be-fore your

ho-ly name. There is joy in heav-en, un-ceas-ing

cel-e-bra-tion, for the Lamb who died has now

**36** | G/D | C | G/B | C | G/B | G

-en, un-ceas - ing joy in your pres - ence; all the

**39** | D | G/D | D | G/D | C | G/B | D

an - gels re-joice when one sin - ner comes back to God.

**42** | G/D | D | G/D

There is joy in heav - en, un - ceas - ing

**45** | C | G/B | C | G/B | Am⁷ | G/B

cel - e - bra - tion by the thou-sands up-on thou-sands washed

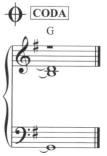

**49** | C | Dsus⁴ | D | C/D D | **D.S.** | CODA | G

in our Sav-ior's blood. Let your

# Lift Up Your Eyes

Ps 107:1, 1Co 15:25-28
Col 2:15, Heb 12:1-3
Rev 5:9-10

Words and Music: Mark Altrogge

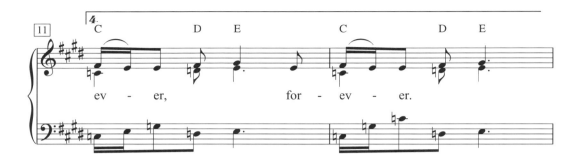

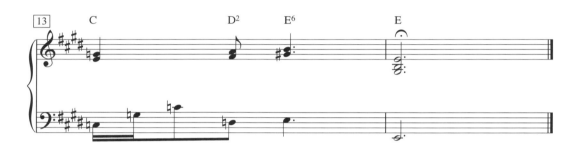

2. Lift up your eyes and see Christ enthroned.
   His mighty cross has vanquished his foes.
   And soon comes a day when to him all will bow.
   And take heart, he will love us forever.

3. Lift up your eyes, his glory proclaim.
   For God has exalted the Lamb that was slain.
   And someday our eyes will look full on his face.
   And take heart, he will love us forever.

4. Lift up your eyes to Christ our High Priest,
   where he has prepared his great wedding feast.
   We'll drink of his joy and rest in his love.
   And take heart, he will love us forever, forever.

# Like a River Glorious

Ps 56:3, Isa 26:3
Col 3:15, Rev 15:13

Words: Frances Havergal (1874)
Music: James Mountain (1876)
Arrangement: Bob Kauflin

# Lord Jesus, Come

*Lord, there is no one like you*

Words and Music: Adam Sacks

1Co 13:12, Php 3:20-22
1Th 4:13-17, Rev 22:20

2. Spirit of God, cleanse my heart;
   rid me of all unbelief,
   while I fix my eyes on the Lamb slain for me.
   We have this glorious hope,
   our great Redeemer's alive;
   as sure as he rose he will come for his bride.

# Lord of the Harvest

## *You came to seek and to save*

Mt 9:37-38, Ac 1:8
Ro 1:3-5

Words and Music: Mark Altrogge

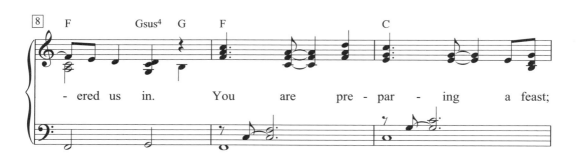

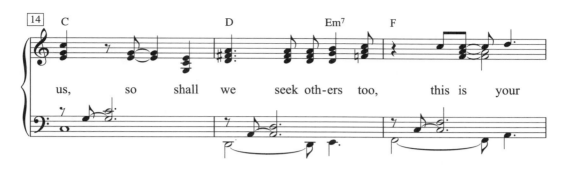

us, so shall we seek oth-ers too, this is your

**CHORUS**

will. For you are the Lord of the har-

- vest, you give the in - crease, you're

build - ing your church. You are the Lord of the har-

# Lord, I Live by Your Word

Dt 8:3, Ps 1:1-6
Isa 55:10-11

Words and Music: Mark Altrogge

bring forth its fruit, so shall be the word that you are

speak-ing. It shall not re-turn

emp-ty to you, it shall ac-com-plish your de-sire, it will

sure-ly suc-ceed; your word trans-forms the des-ert, and your

Word is chang-ing me.

I live by your Word.

# Make His Praise Great

Ps 29:1-2, Ps 66:2
Ps 96:1-4, Ps 99:2-3

Words and Music: Mark Altrogge

Make his praise great and glo - ri - ous, Je - sus reigns all
King of kings, Lord of right - eous - ness, we shall bring you

vic - to - ri - ous; gra - cious God, rul - ing o - ver us,
the ve - ry best; Je - sus come, be our hon - ored guest,

there is no one like you!
there is no one like you!

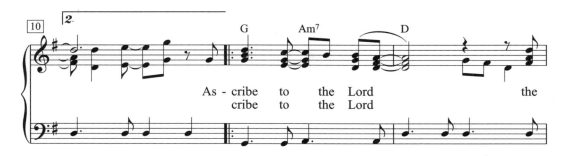

As - cribe to the Lord the
cribe to the Lord

# May Thy Kingdom Come

Ps 67:1-2, Mt 6:9-10

Words and Music: Marsha Dixon Brown

1. May thy king-dom come in all the

earth, may thy will be done

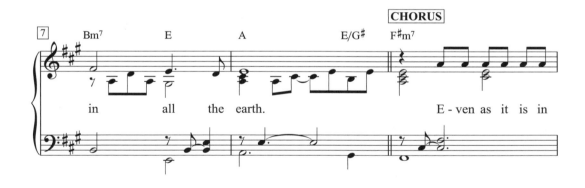

in all the earth. E-ven as it is in

heav-en, so bring it to the earth;

2. May thy power come in all the earth,
   may thy power come in all the earth.

# Mercies Anew
## *Every morning that breaks*
### Words and Music: Mark Altrogge and Bob Kauflin

Ps 13:6, Ps 136:1
Lam 3:22-23, Ro 8:28
2Co 1:3-4

♩ = 100

**VERSE**

1. Ev-'ry morn - ing that breaks there are mer - - cies a-
   fal - len and strayed there were mer - - cies a-
   storms swirl and rage, there are mer - - cies a-

new. Ev-'ry breath that I take is your faith - ful - ness
new. For you sought me in love and my heart you pur-
new. In af - flic - tion and pain, you will car - ry me

proved, and at the end of each day, when my la - bors are
sued. In the face of my sin, Lord, you nev - er with-
through. And at the end of my days, when your throne fills my

last time to coda

through, I will sing of your mer - cies a - new.
drew. I will sing of your mer - cies a - new.
view, I will sing of your mer - cies a -

2. When I've     And your

# Mighty God

Ps 110:1, 1Co 15:24-25
Eph 1:20-23, Php 2:9-11
1Ti 6:15

Words and Music: Mark Altrogge

Might-y God, King of kings, un-dis-put-ed Lord of

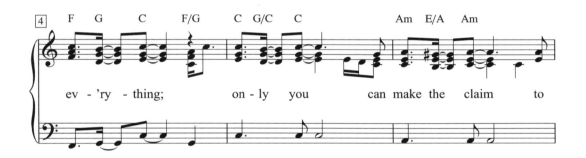

ev-'ry-thing; on-ly you can make the claim to

have the Name a-bove all oth-er names.

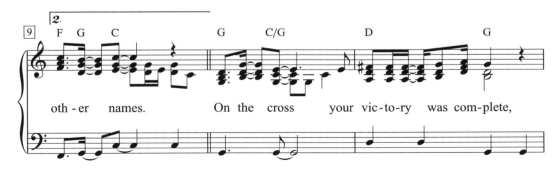

oth-er names. On the cross your vic-to-ry was com-plete,

# Mighty, Mighty Savior
## *No one is good*

Ps 51:2-10, Ac 4:12
Ro 3:10-12, Ro 7:15-25

### Words and Music: Mark Altrogge

for help-less sin - ners like me. What a

**CHORUS**

might-y, might-y Sav - ior you are. What a

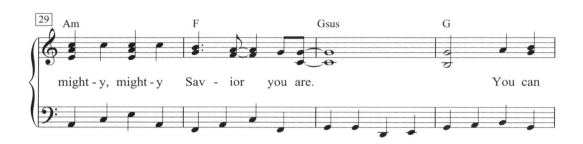

might-y, might-y Sav - ior you are. You can

wash a-way my sin. You can change my heart with-in. What a

might-y, might-y Sav - ior you are.

# More and More Like You

*Lord, change my heart*

Words and Music: Bob Kauflin

Ro 6:11-14, Ro 12:1-2
Ro 13:14, 1Co 10:13
Php 2:12-13

Prayerfully

1. Lord, change my heart from deep with-in, pu-ri-fy me once a-
   will to choose your ways in each temp-ta-tion that I

gain, re-new my mind to love your truth;
face, un-til your glo-ry's shin-ing through;
make me more and more like

**CHORUS**

you. More and more like you, more and more like

you. Do what-ev - er you must do to make me more and more like

you.

2. Lord, cause my

# More of You

## *More of you and less of me*

Words and Music: Bob Kauflin

Jn 3:30, Ro 6:11-14
Gal 2:20, Eph 5:1-2
2Ti 2:20-21

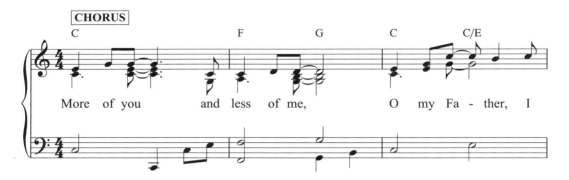

More of you and less of me, O my Fa - ther, I

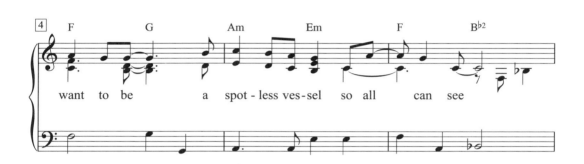

want to be a spot - less ves - sel so all can see

more of you and less of me.

1. What can I of - fer you when the ver - y best I do is

# More Than Life Itself

## *My soul finds rest in you alone*

Ps 62:1-2, Ps 63:1-3
Ps 73:25-26, Ps 139:16
Php 1:20-23

Words and Music: Steve & Vikki Cook

1. My soul finds rest in you a-lone, you are the
2. My soul finds joy in you a-lone, you are my

God who knows my ways. Your sov-'reign-ty is so
foun-tain of de-lights. The men-tion of your

sweet to me; in your hands are all my days.
match-less name caus-es my heart to soar on high. More than

# My Father

Ps 27:4, Ps 73:25-26
Isa 63:16, Ro 5:10
Ro 8:15

Words and Music: Steve & Vikki Cook

VERSE

My Fa - ther, I rest as a child in your arms, con - tent in your pre - sence and qui - et in heart. My on - ly de - sire is to be where you are, find - ing my joy in your

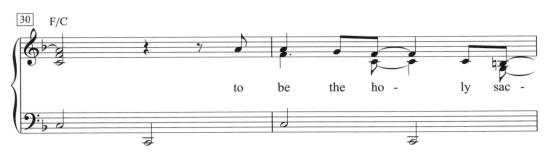

to be the ho - ly sac -

- ri - fice        that gives

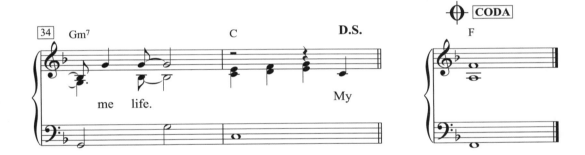

me life.        My

# My Glorious Hope
## *Though waves of troubles come*

Words and Music: Steve & Vikki Cook

Hab 3:17-18, Ro 15:13
Jas 1:12, 1Pe 1:3-9
1Pe 5:10

# My Glory and the One Who Lifts My Head

## *Sovereign God*

Ps 3:3, Ps 65:5-8
Ps 73:28

Words and Music: Mark Altrogge

# No God but God

Ps 90:1-2, Ps 145:13
Isa 45:18, Isa 45:22-23

Words and Music: Bob Kauflin

No God but God, no cre-a-tor but the Lord our Mak-er. No God but God, the great I Am. E-ter-nal and com-plete, we wor-ship at his feet, for-ev-er there will be no God but God.

# No Sacrifice
## *I have found my treasure*

Ps 16:11, Mt 6:19-21
Mt 13:45-46, Php 3:7-11

Words and Music: Mark Altrogge

of sur-ren-der-ing all. It is no sac-ri-fice to give up all for you, for-sak-ing things I can-not keep to gain what I can't lose. It is no sac-ri-fice for you are un-sur-passed in beau-ty and sweet-ness and splen-dor.

2. I have found such pleasure in knowing you, my God.
Blessings without measure and riches without cost.
But when contentment dulls my heart and comforts dim my view,
Lord, rekindle holy passions and the joy of following you.

# Not to Us

Ps 96:1-4, Ps 115:1

Words and Music: Mark Altrogge

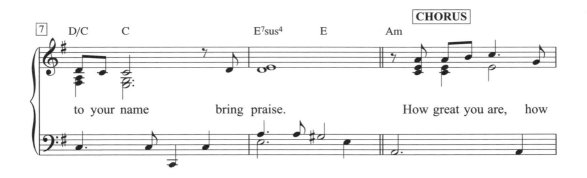

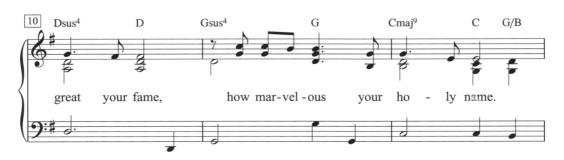

We are but ser - vants who pro - claim your per -

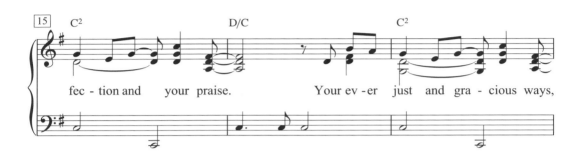

fec - tion and your praise. Your ev - er just and gra - cious ways,

how ex - cel - lent you are, O Lord.

# O Faithful God

## *I will praise you all my life*

Dt 7:9, Ps 146:1-5
Lam 3:58, 1Co 1:9

Words and Music: Mark Altrogge

up and you up-hold my cause; you give me

life, you dry my eyes, you're al - ways

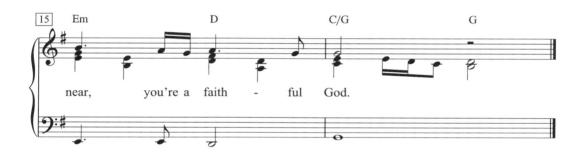

near, you're a faith - ful God.

# O Give Thanks

Ps 118:1, Ps 118:6-7
Ps 118:15-16

Words and Music: Mark Altrogge

# O God, My God

Ps 63:1-8

Words and Music: Bob Kauflin

# O God, Our Help in Ages Past

Ps 61:4, Ps 90

Original words: Isaac Watts
Alt. words, chorus and music: Mark Altrogge

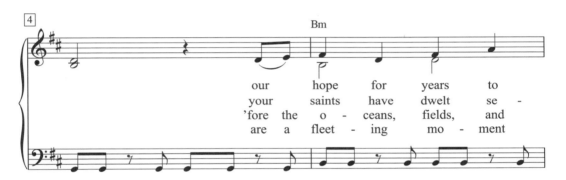

# O Most High
## *I will give thanks*

Words and Music: Mark Altrogge

Ps 9:1-2, 9-10
Heb 13:8

I will give thanks to the Lord with all my heart, I will sing

glo - ri - ous prais - es to your name.

I will be glad and ex-ult in you, my Lord. Yes - ter-

day, to-day, for-ev - er, you're the same.

**CHORUS**

**17** Am G F Dm⁷ G C

O Most High, you who are my strong-hold, when

**21** Am G F Dm⁷ Gsus⁴ G

trou-bles come, you're my hid-ing-place.

**25** Am G F Dm⁷ G C

O Most High, those who know you, trust you, and

**29** Am G F Dm⁷ G⁷ C G/C

you will not for-sake the ones who seek your face.

**33** F/C G/C C

# O Wondrous Love

Dt 1:31, Dt 33:27
Ps 100:5, Ro 8:38-39
Php 3:12

Words and Music: Steve & Vikki Cook

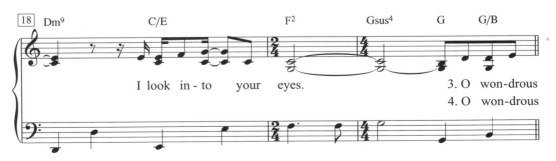

# Once This Heart

Eze 36:26-27, Ro 2:4
Ro 6:17-18

Words and Music: Mark Altrogge

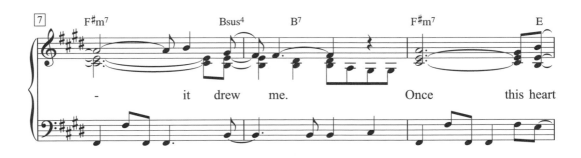

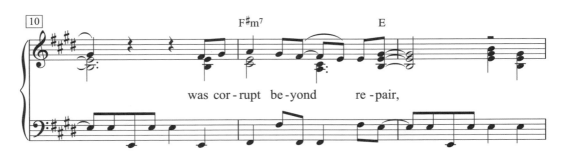

# One Pure and Holy Passion

*Give me one pure and holy passion*

Words and Music: Mark Altrogge

Ps 27:4, Ps 73:25-26
Php 3:7-14

Give me one pure and ho - ly pas - sion,

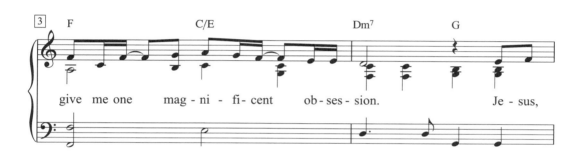

give me one mag - ni - fi - cent ob - ses - sion. Je - sus,

give me one glo - ri - ous am - bi - tion for my life to

know and fol - low hard af - ter you. To

**CHORUS**

know and fol-low hard af - ter you, to

grow as your dis-ci - ple in the truth. This world is

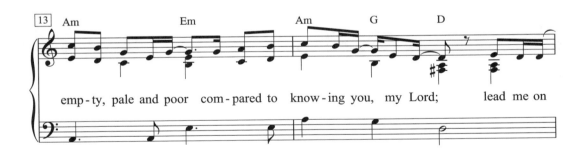

emp-ty, pale and poor com-pared to know-ing you, my Lord; lead me on

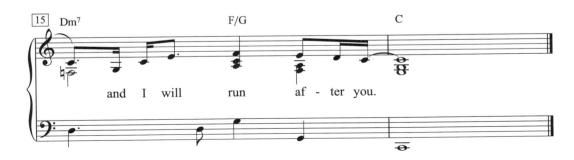

and I will run af - ter you.

# Only in the Cross

## *When I look upon the cross*

Words and Music: Mark Altrogge

1Co 1:18, 1Co 1:23
2Co 5:21, Gal 6:14

**VERSE**

1. When I look up-on the cross in that

spec-ta-cle of suf-fer-ing I see the pow-er of God.

There the Son of God was crushed and

lift-ed up to die for me and con-quered death for-ev-er.

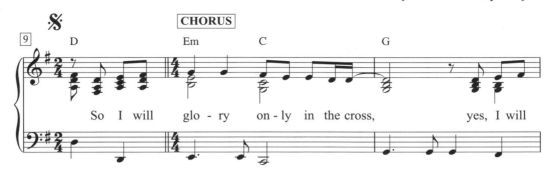

**CHORUS**

So I will glo - ry on - ly in the cross, yes, I will

glo - ry on - ly in the cross and I will

make my boast in the Lord Je - sus Christ cru - ci - fied

to ran - som us.

**VERSE**

2. When I look up - on the cross, in

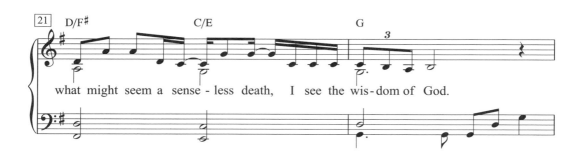

what might seem a sense - less death, I see the wis - dom of God.

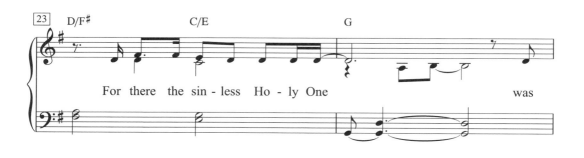

For there the sin - less Ho - ly One was

made to be sin for me, then he de - clared me righ - teous.

# Only You for Me

## *When the cares of life come*

Ps 73:25-26, Hab 3:17-18
Ro 8:35-39, Heb 12:1-3

Words and Music: Steve & Vikki Cook

No oth-er god will I ev-er seek, I

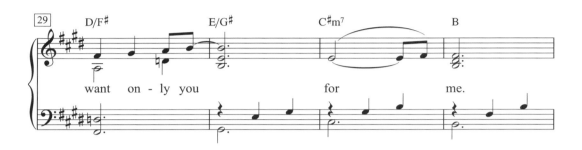

want on-ly you for me.

Through all of e-ter-ni-ty

there'll be on-ly you for me.

2. When the

3. As I run the race I will hope in your grace;
there's only you for me.
When my flesh has failed and I step through the veil;
there's only you for me.
And I'll fully know that you're all I need.

# Open Our Eyes

2Co 4:2-4, Eph 1:16-21
Eph 2:4-7

Words and Music: Mark Altrogge

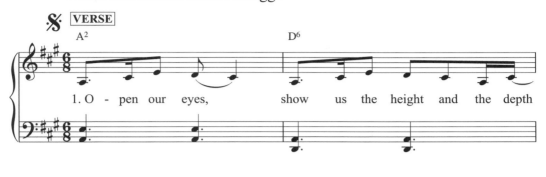

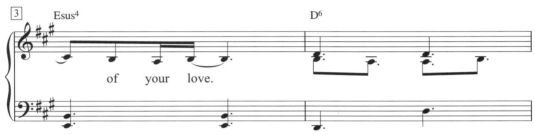

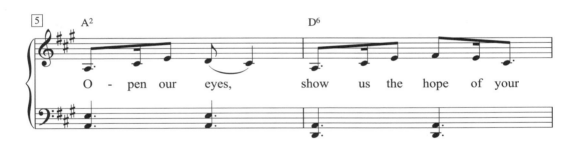

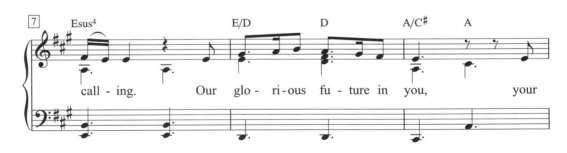

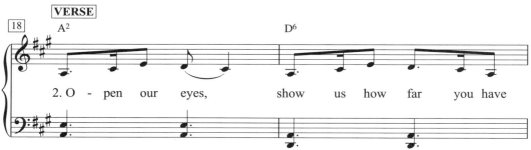

**VERSE**

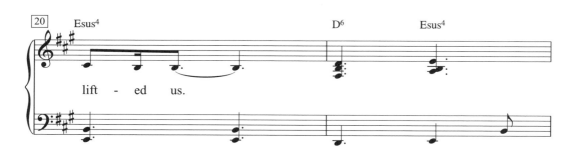

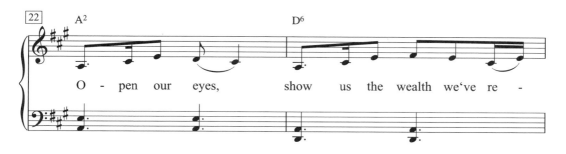

# Perfect Lamb of God
## *The light of day*

Lk 23:44-47, Jn 1:29
Ro 5:6-11, Col 2:13-15
Rev 5:11-14

### Words and Music: Adam Sacks

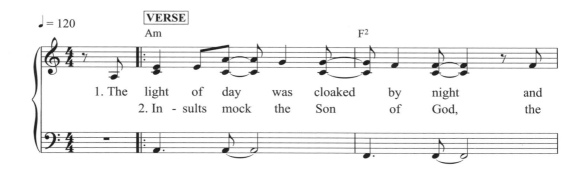

1. The light of day was cloaked by night and
2. In-sults mock the Son of God, and the

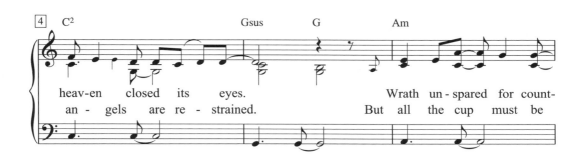

heav-en closed its eyes. Wrath un-spared for count-
an-gels are re-strained. But all the cup must be

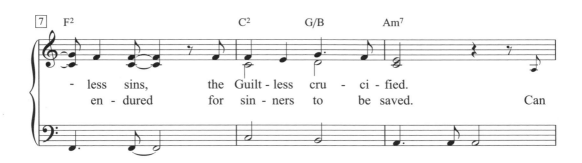

-less sins, the Guilt-less cru-ci-fied.
en-dured for sin-ners to be saved. Can

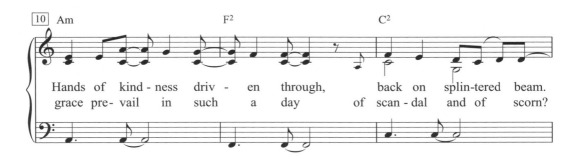

Hands of kind-ness driv-en through, back on splin-tered beam.
grace pre-vail in such a day of scan-dal and of scorn?

# Pleasing in Your Sight

Pr 8:27-31, Jn 17:24
Php 2:6-8

Words and Music: Mark Altrogge

# Praise God

Verse 1: Thomas Ken, Verses 2 & 3: Isaac Watts
Alt. words, verse 1: Bob Kauflin
Music from Louis Bourgeois' Genevan Psalter
Arranged: Bob Kauflin

Ps 100, Ps 150
Php 2:9-11

# Raise Up an Army

Ps 96:3, Mt 28:18-20
Ac 1:8, Rev 14:6

Words and Music: Steve & Vikki Cook

2. Oh God, our glorious maker,
   we marvel at your grace,
   that you would use us in your plan,
   rejoicing at your favor,
   delighting in your ways,
   we'll gladly follow your command.

# Receive the Glory
## *Not to us*

Words and Music: Bob Kauflin

Ps 115:1, Isa 26:12
Isa 43:1, 2Co 4:7
Php 3:3

Not to us, but to your name a - lone, be all the glo - ry, the glo - ry, for - ev - er. For your faith - ful-ness and stead - fast love, re - ceive the glo-ry. The glo - ry be - longs to you.

**last time to coda**

**VERSE**

1. All that we've ac - com-plished you have done for us. And
2. On - ly by your mer - cy can we come to you. Though

# Rock of Ages, Cleft for Me

Words: Augustus M. Toplady
Alt. words: Bob Kauflin
Music: Bob Kauflin

Ps 18:2, Ps 51:2
Ro 3:19-20, Gal 2:16-21

1. Rock of ag - es cleft for me, let me hide my - self in thee. Let the wa - ter and the blood, from thy wound - ed side which flowed, be of sin the dou - ble cure, save from wrath and make me pure.

2. All the la - bors of my hands could not meet thy law's de - mands. Could my zeal no res - pite know? Could my tears for - ev - er flow? All for sin could not a - tone. Thou must save, and thou a - lone.

3. Noth - ing in my hands I bring. Simp - ly to thy cross I cling. Na - ked, come to thee for dress. Help - less, look to thee for grace. To thy foun - tain, Lord I fly. Wash me Sav - ior, or I die.

4. While I draw this fleet - ing breath, when my eyes shall close in death, when I soar to worlds un - known, see thee on thy judg - ment throne. Rock of ag - es, cleft for me. Let me hide my - self in thee.

# Shout

Ps 32:11, 1Th 4:16-17
2Th 1:9-10, Rev 19:9

**Words and Music: Mark Altrogge**

With drive CHORUS

Shout, lift a shout, a might-y shout to the King. Shout, lift a shout, might-y shout to the King.

Lord, our fa - ces are ra - diant with a ho - ly joy. We love to sing of your free grace and dy - ing love. We will shout to you, we will

# Show Me Your Glory

Ex 33:17-19, Ex 34:6-8
Ps 73:28

Words and Music: Mark Altrogge

1. Lord show me your glo - ry, cause
show me your glo - ry, your

all of your good - ness to pass be - fore my
sov - 'reign com - pas - sion, your ho - ly wrath toward

eyes. Lord show me your glo - ry pro -
sin. Lord show me your glo - ry, your

2nd verse melody

choose to show to

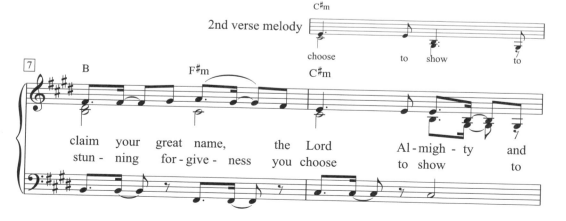

claim your great name, the Lord Al - migh - ty and
stun - ning for - give - ness you choose to show to

# Showers of Mercy

Ex 33:17-19, Ac 3:19-21

Words and Music: Mark Altrogge

Show-ers of mer - cy and riv - ers of bless - ing,

show-ers of mer - cy and times of re - fresh - ing,

show-ers of mer - cy that flow from your pres - ence, O

Lord, re - vive us once more.

last time to coda

# Soli Deo Gloria

*We resolve to know nothing else*

Words and Music: Mark Altrogge

Ps 108:5, Isa 42:8
1Co 2:2, Rev 15:4

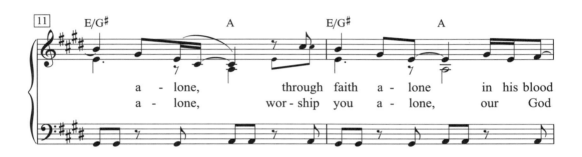

**CHORUS**

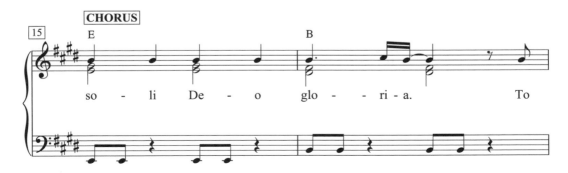

God a - lone be glo - ry, to God a - lone be glo - ry. Sing - ing

so - li De - o glo - ri - a. To

God a - lone be glo - ry, to God a - lone be glo - ry

in Je - sus Christ. 2. We re -

# Song of the Lamb
## *Long ago*

Words and Music: Mark Altrogge

Ps 63:4, Ps 103:17
Isa 59:1-2, Hos 11:4
Php 2:8-11, Rev 15:3

Lyrics:

1. Long a-go, be-fore you made the stars a-bove, you set your ev-er-last-ing love on us, and your love en-dures. With ten-der chords, you drew us who had strayed so far, and like a might-y war-rior

2. All our sins have made a chasm deep and wide; we could nev-er reach the oth-er side till you came to save. O glo-rious God, emp-tied to be-come like us, a hum-ble ser-vant tak-ing

# Sovereign One
## *When I'm all alone*

Words and Music: Zach Jones

Ps 23:4, Ps 25:1-7
Isa 40:12

1. When I'm all a-lone and a-
   don't get to have my own

fraid, I will trust in you, for you watch o-ver my
way, I will trust in you, for you know what is

ways. When things in my life don't make
best. When tears be-gin to roll down my

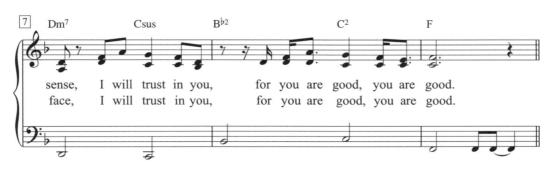

sense, I will trust in you, for you are good, you are good.
face, I will trust in you, for you are good, you are good.

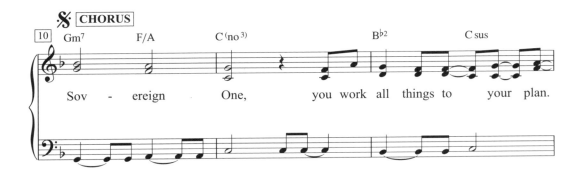

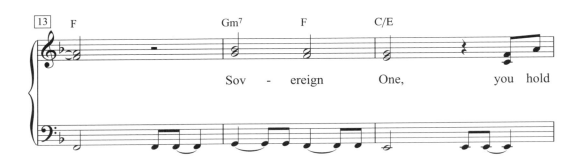

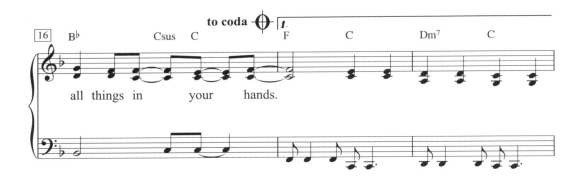

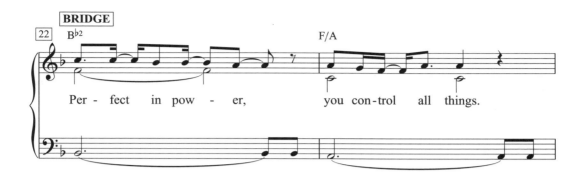

# Surrender All

*Take all I am, Lord*

Words and Music: Rich Dalmas

Ps 139: 23-24, Lk 14:33
2Co 7:1, Jas 4:10

# Thank You for the Cross

Ac 20:28, 1Co 1:18,
2Co 3:18, Gal 6:14
Col 1:19-20

Words and Music: Mark Altrogge

Thank you for the cross, the might - y cross that

God him - self would die for such as us, and

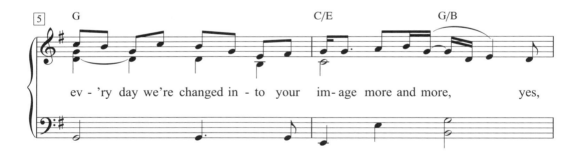

ev - 'ry day we're changed in - to your im - age more and more, yes,

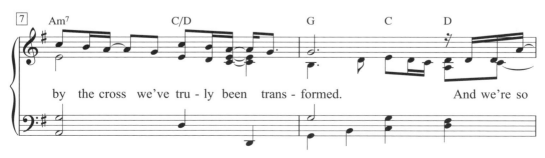

by the cross we've tru - ly been trans - formed. And we're so

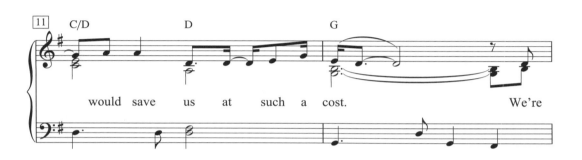

# That I Might Gain Christ

*What I once called gain*

Words and Music: Dave Fournier

Ps 86:11, 1Co 9:24-26
Php 1:21, Php 3:7-11
Col 3:1-4

With a strong rhythm

1. What I once called gain  I will count as  loss,  I've been cap-ti-va-

-ted by  the cross.  You steal my breath a-way  with that dis-play of  love,

I want to see the  face  of your glo-ri-ous Son.  Lord,  be  my

sin-gle vi-sion;  I'll run my race  to re-ceive my crown.

But you are the great-est gift I've been giv-en, help me lay all my

**CHORUS**

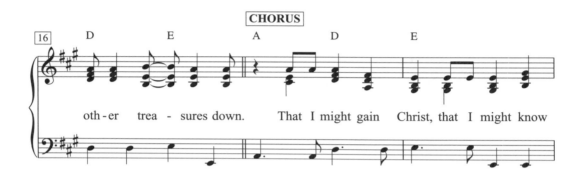

oth-er trea-sures down. That I might gain Christ, that I might know

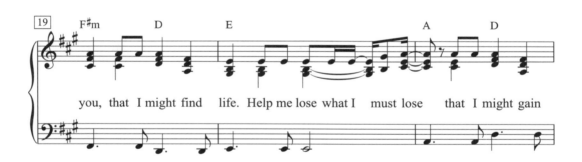

you, that I might find life. Help me lose what I must lose that I might gain

to coda

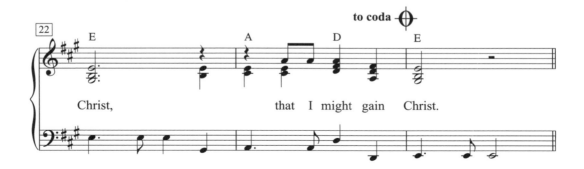

Christ, that I might gain Christ.

# The Almighty God Is with Me
## *Though the mountains fall*

Ps 27:1-3, Ps 46:1-3
Ps 91:1, Ps 118:6-9

Words and Music: Steve & Vikki Cook

1. Though the moun - tains fall in - to the sea and the
   ar - mies would come a - gainst me from the

earth gives way. Though the wa - ters come
east and west. Though a thou - sand would

in like a flood, I will not be dis - mayed.
fall at my side, I will know his rest.

God is my ref - uge. God is my

ref - uge and my strength, my strength. The Al-

# The Audience of One
## *I have one passion*

Words and Music: Steve & Vikki Cook

Mt 25:23, Mk 12:30
2Co 5:14-15, Php 3:14
1Th 2:11-12

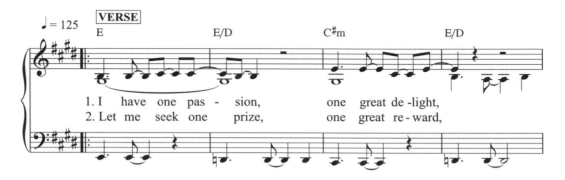

1. I have one pas - sion, one great de -light,
2. Let me seek one prize, one great re - ward,

one cen - ter of my life,
one hope I trea - sure most,

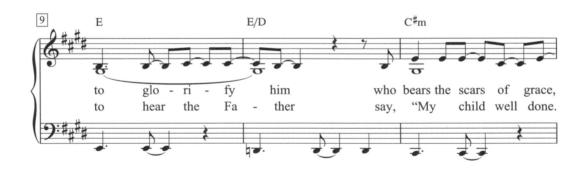

to glo - ri - fy him who bears the scars of grace,
to hear the Fa - ther say, "My child well done.

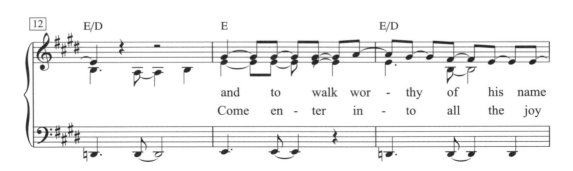

and to walk wor - thy of his name
Come en - ter in - to all the joy

for all my days.
found in my Son."

**CHORUS**

With all my heart and soul and strength, in ev - 'ry

word and thought and deed, I'll live for him who died for me,

to please the Au - di - ence of One. How can I

not pledge all my love, in light of

all that he has done? There is one glo - ry that I seek:

to please the Au - di - ence of One.

# The Glories of Calvary

*Lord, you're calling me to come*

Words and Music: Steve & Vikki Cook

Ps 96:2, Ro 5:20-21
Gal 6:14, Col 1:25-27
Heb 12:22-24

1. Lord, you're call - - ing me to come and be - hold
e - ter - nal joy in the tri -

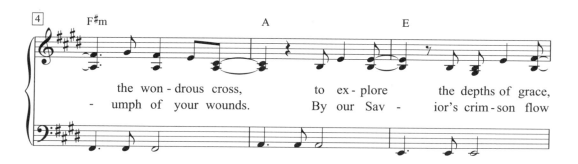

the won - drous cross, to ex - plore the depths of grace,
- umph of your wounds. By our Sav - ior's crim - son flow

that came to me at such a cost. Where your
ho - ly wrath has been re - moved. And your

bound - - - less love con-quered my
saints be - low join with your

# The Glory of the Ages

*Jesus, how we love you*

Words and Music: Steve & Vikki Cook

Ps 36:9, Php 2:9-11
1Ti 1:17, Heb 1:8-12
Rev 5:11-13

# The Glory of the Cross
## *What wisdom once devised*

Ro 3:19-26, Ro 4:1-8
Ro 11:32-36, 2Co 5:21
Php 3:7-11, 1Jn 4:9-10

Words and Music: Bob Kauflin

**VERSE**

1. What wis-dom once de-vised the plan where all our sin and pride was

placed up-on the per-fect Lamb who suf-fered, bled, and died? The

wis-dom of a sov-'reign God whose great-ness will be shown, when

those who cru-ci-fied your Son re-joice a-round your throne.

**CHORUS**

And oh, the glo-ry of the cross; that

2. What righteousness was there revealed
   that sets the guilty free,
   that justifies ungodly men
   and calls the filthy clean?
   A righteousness that proved to all
   your justice has been met,
   and holy wrath is satisfied
   through one atoning death.

3. What mercy now has been proclaimed
   for those who would believe;
   a love incomprehensible,
   our minds could not conceive?
   A mercy that forgives my sin
   and makes me like your Son,
   and now I'm loved forevermore
   because of what you've done.

# The Glory of the Lamb

## *A day is coming*

Words and Music: Mark Altrogge

Ps 102:25-27, 1Co 13:12
2Ti 4:8, 2Pe 3:13
Rev 1:22-23, Rev 22:5

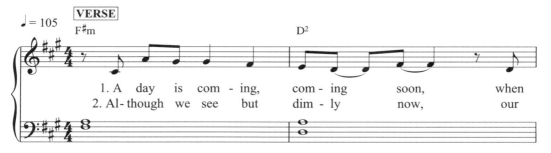

1. A day is com-ing, com-ing soon, when
2. Al-though we see but dim-ly now, our

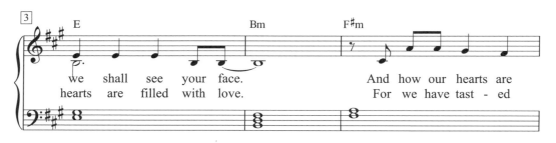

we shall see your face. And how our hearts are
hearts are filled with love. For we have tast-ed

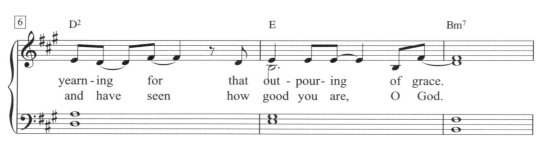

yearn-ing for that out-pour-ing of grace.
and have seen how good you are, O God.

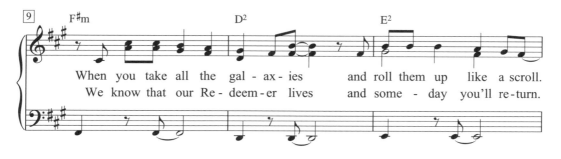

When you take all the gal-ax-ies and roll them up like a scroll.
We know that our Re-deem-er lives and some-day you'll re-turn.

When you make Heav'n and Earth a-new and e-
And we shall see you with our eyes, oh

# The Gospel Song

### *Holy God, in love, became*

Words: Drew Jones
Music: Bob Kauflin

Mt 1:23, 1Co 15:3-4
2Co 5:21, Eph 2:1-7
Heb 7:26, 1Pe 2:24

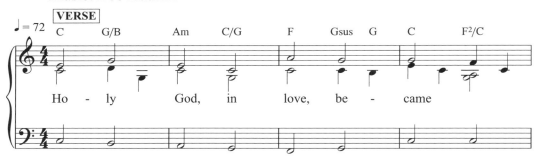

Ho - ly God, in love, be - came

per - fect Man to bear my blame.

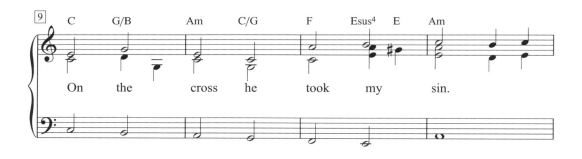

On the cross he took my sin.

By his death I live a - gain.

# The Highest Glory

Php 2:8-11

Words and Music: Mark Altrogge

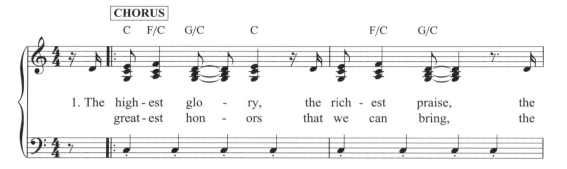

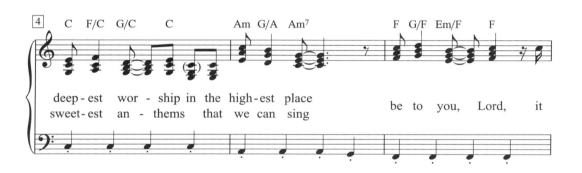

# The Hope of Glory
## *Thank you, Lord*

Col 1:26-28, 1Th 3:12-14
1Jn 3:2

**Words and Music: Mark Altrogge**

Thank you, Lord, for this hope in me, the hope of glo-

-ry, the hope of glo - ry. Thank you, Lord, for this

hope in me, the hope of glo - ry, the hope of glo - ry.

Christ in me, Christ in me, con-form-ing me to your

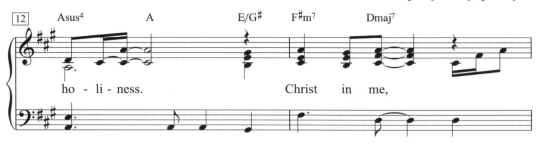

ho - li - ness.        Christ  in  me,

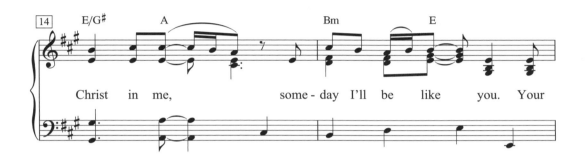

Christ  in  me,        some - day I'll  be  like  you.  Your

face  I  will  see;    you're  my  hope of  glo - ry, Christ  in  me.

# The Look

## *I saw one hanging on a tree*

Isa 53, 2Co 5:21

Original words: John Newton
Music and alt. words: Bob Kauflin

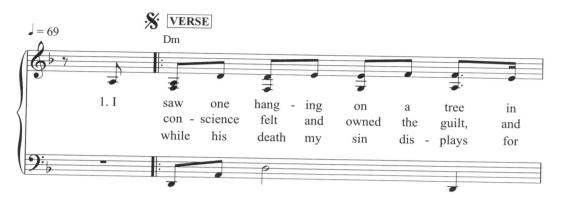

1. I saw one hang-ing on a tree in
con - science felt and owned the guilt, and
while his death my sin dis - plays and for

ag - o - ny and blood, who fixed his lov - ing eyes on me, as
plunged me in de - spair. I saw my sins his blood had spilt, and
all the world to view, such is the mys - ter - y of grace: it

near his cross I stood. And nev - er till my dy - ing breath will
helped to nail him there. But with a sec - ond look he said "I
seals my par -don, too. With pleas -ing grief and mourn-ful joy, my

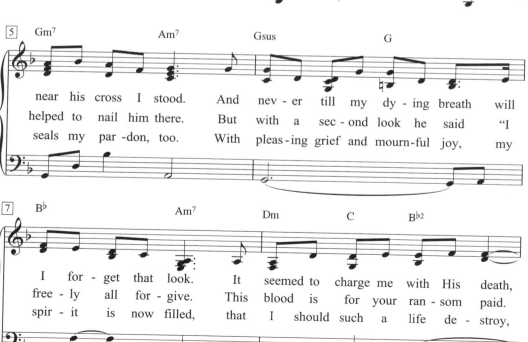

I for - get that look. It seemed to charge me with His death,
free - ly all for - give. This blood is for your ran - som paid.
spir - it is now filled, that I should such a life de - stroy,

grace,    that  looked  on  me  and  glad - ly  took   my

place.

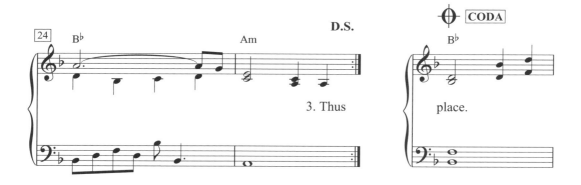

3. Thus           place.

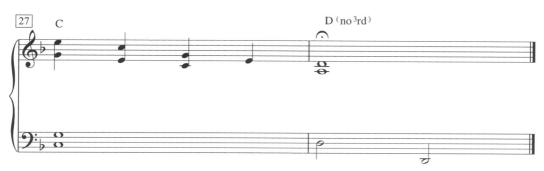

# The Love of a Holy God
## *How lovely you are*

Ps 5:4-7, Ps 34:8-9
Ps 84:1-2

Words and Music: Mark Altrogge

1. How love - ly you are.
love - ly you are.

I mar - vel at your beau - ty.
Your hands still bear the nail marks.

I'm rav - ished by one glance from your lov - ing eyes.
I see your wound - ed side that was pierced for me.

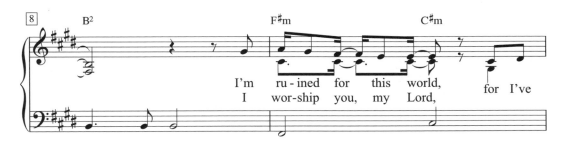

I'm ru - ined for this world,
I wor - ship you, my Lord, for I've

tast-ed your love, the love of a ho - ly God. No

# The Most Wonderful of All
## *Soaring mountains*

Ps 102:25-27, Ro 1:18-25
Heb 1:3-14

Words and Music: Mark Altrogge and Steve Cook

fall down on our knees at one glimpse of your maj - es - ty

for you are the most won-der-ful of all.

2. The

2. The glorious planets, the fiery lights,
  the jewelled heavens that adorn the night.
  Even flaming angels and seraphim
  all pale before your splendor, O Lord,
  for you're the most wonderful of all.

# The One and Only God
## *You are the one and only God*

Ps 19:1-3, Ps 33:13-17
Isa 40:17-18, Isa 43:7
Isa 45:18, 21

Words and Music: Bob Kauflin

You are the one and on-ly God.

No one com-pares to who you are.

You're the first and you're the last,

you know the fu-ture from the past. You're the

Mak - er and Re - deem - er of our hearts,

you are the one and on - ly God.

**last time to coda**

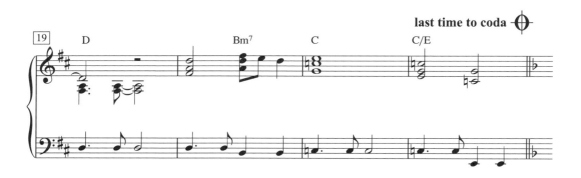

**VERSE**

1. You hold the na - tions in your hands. King-doms rise
2. Through - out the u - ni - verse you've made, your

# The Power and the Glory

## *Never has a death*

Ro 5:15, Ro 6:23
1Co 1:18-25, 1Co 2:1-5

Words and Music: Mark Altrogge

**VERSE**

1. Nev-er has a death meant so much to so man-y, and

nev-er has a death changed so man-y lives.

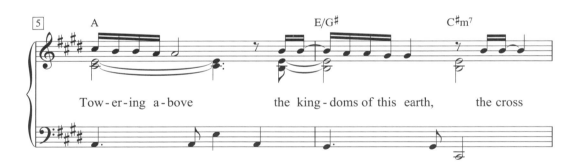

Tow-er-ing a-bove the king-doms of this earth, the cross

casts its might-y shad-ow o-ver his-to-ry and na-

# The Prize of My Life

## *My Father, how you care for me*

Ps 145:15-19, Ro 8:15
Php 3:8, Php 3:14

Words and Music: Steve & Vikki Cook

1. My Fa - ther, how you care for me, fill - ing my life with good. Your faith - ful ways bring hope and peace day af - ter day. There is none who com - pares with you on the earth or the skies a - bove. Lord, I long to be near

to you, you're my great - est joy, my high - est love.

**CHORUS**

You are my glo - ri - ous prize. Fa - ther, you are the pas - sion that fills

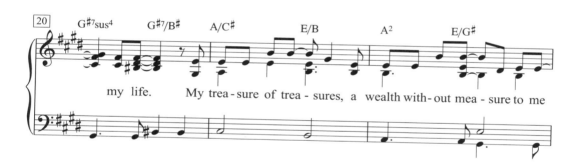

my life. My trea - sure of trea - sures, a wealth with - out mea - sure to me

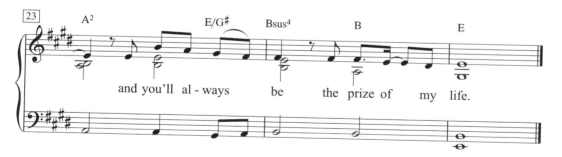

and you'll al - ways be the prize of my life.

2. My Father, draw me to your side.
   For you are my soul's delight.
   To hear your voice, to know your heart,
   my burning desire.
   There is none who compares with you
   on the earth or the skies above.
   Lord, I long to be near to you,
   you're my greatest joy,
   my highest love.

# Then Your Grace Appeared

## *All of us like sheep had gone*

Isa 53:6, Eph 2:13
Titus 2:11-14, Titus 3:3-7

Words and Music: Mark Altrogge

1. All of us like sheep had gone a-stray. Each of us had turned to his own way. Chil-dren of wrath and strife, who'd nev-er known the path of life, with-out an-y hope in the world. But then your

2. All of us had cold and ston-y hearts. Stum-bl-ing and grop-ing in the dark. Snared and en-slaved by sin, pur-su-ing our own self-ish ends, con-sumed by un-ho-ly de-sires.

# There Is No One Like Our God

## *His hands spread out the heavens*

Words and Music: Steve & Vikki Cook

Ps 104:2-3, Ps 145:1-6
Isa 46:5-10, Isa 57:15
1Jn 3:1

1. His hands spread out the heav-ens and set the stars in
2. He is the King of glo-ry, whose reign will nev-er

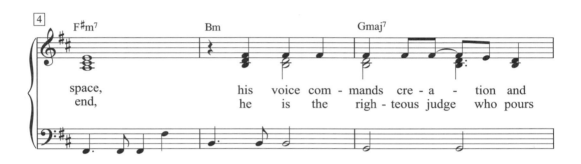

space, his voice com-mands cre-a-tion and
end, he is the righ-teous judge who pours

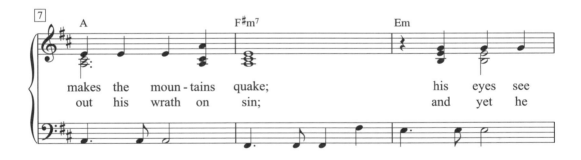

makes the moun-tains quake; his eyes see
out his wrath on sin; and yet he

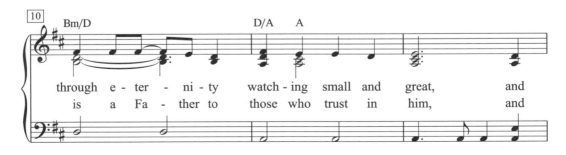

through e-ter-ni-ty watch-ing small and great, and
is a Fa-ther to those who trust in him, and

he        is  our  God.
he        is  our  God.

**CHORUS**

There  is    no    one      like our    God,

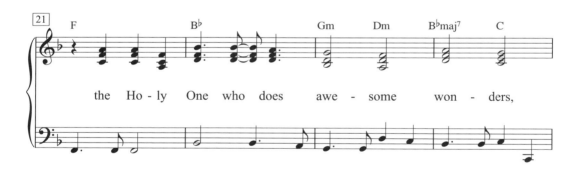

the  Ho - ly   One  who  does   awe - some      won - ders,

there  is    no    one    like our    God.          Give  him  the

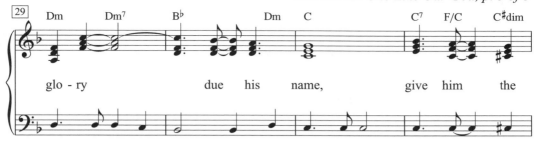

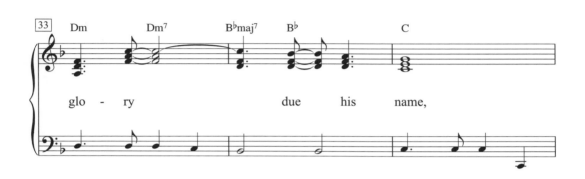

# There Is One Thing

Ps 27:4, 1Jn 3:1-2

Words and Music: Mark Altrogge

# This Fathomless Love

*Lord, what moved your heart*

Words and Music: Steve & Vikki Cook

Isa 53:3, Jn 10:14-15
Ro 5:5-8, Gal 3:13
Eph 1:4, Eph 3:14-19

**VERSE**

1. Lord, what moved your heart to love low - ly man
   and take as your own

be - fore a - ny star could her - ald your
those who had crushed your one pre - cious

praise, and why did you come a - bas - ing your-self,
Son, why mer - cy and grace towards your en - e - mies;

veiled in a robe of frail hu - man
your name they have cursed and your throne they have

clay? Why would you, the pure, give your
shunned? Oh how could you choose to show

# This I Know

Ps 56:9, Ro 8:28-34
Heb 4:16, Heb 7:25

Words and Music: Mark Altrogge

# Those Who Know Their God

Dan 11:32, Php 3:8-11
Eph 6:16-18, Heb 4:12

Words and Music: Mark Altrogge

**VERSE**

Those who know their God will grow strong-er ev-'ry day.

You've chos-en us, O God, and re-

vealed to us your ways. We take the shield of faith

and quench all fi-ery darts. We

wield the might-y sword of your Word that

# Three in One
## *Gracious Father*
### Words and Music: Mark Altrogge

Mt 28:19, Jn 3:16
Jn 16:12-15, Eph 1:4-6
Php 2:6-11

♩=85  VERSE

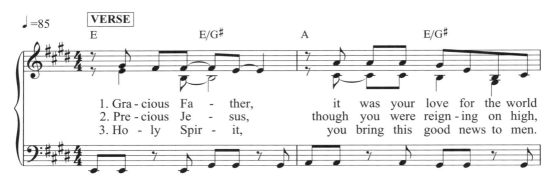

1. Gra-cious Fa - ther, it was your love for the world
2. Pre-cious Je - sus, though you were reign-ing on high,
3. Ho - ly Spir - it, you bring this good news to men.

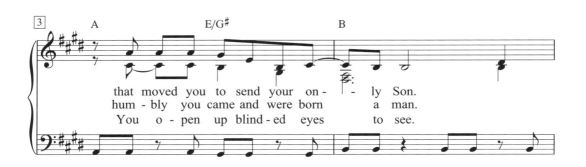

that moved you to send your on - ly Son.
hum - bly you came and were born a man.
You o - pen up blind-ed eyes to see.

Gra-cious Fa - ther, this was your plan from all time,
Pre-cious Je - sus, you were the ser - vant of all.
Ho - ly Spir - it, come now and o - pen my heart.

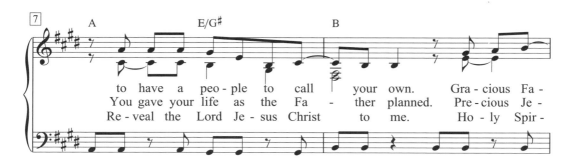

to have a peo-ple to call your own. Gra-cious Fa -
You gave your life as the Fa - ther planned. Pre-cious Je -
Re - veal the Lord Je - sus Christ to me. Ho - ly Spir -

# To Be with You
## *I do not seek*

Ps 105:4, Php 1:21-23
Php 3:7-11, 2Ti 4:8

Words and Music: Steve & Vikki Cook

**VERSE**

I do not seek the wealth of this world, but the
rich-es I find at your feet. I do not long for the
glo-ries of the earth, but the splen-dor that your pres-ence brings.
I de-sire to be with you, the e-ter-
nal, Ho-ly One. **CHORUS** To be with you, to be with

# Treasured Possession
## *You're not ashamed*

Words and Music: Mark Altrogge

Ex 19:5, Zech 2:8
Heb 2:10-13, Heb 10:19-22

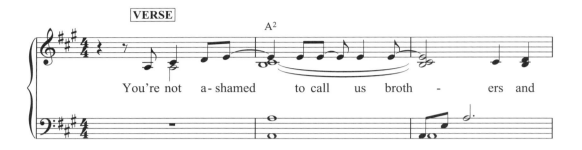

You're not a-shamed to call us broth - ers and

sis - ters, not a-shamed to call us your

own. Not a-shamed to bring us near to the Fa-

ther, for by your blood we come to your

# Triumph of the Crucified
## *We share in the triumph*

Ro 8:33-35, 1Co 15:54-57
Col 3:1-4, 1Pe 5:1

Words and Music: Mark Altrogge

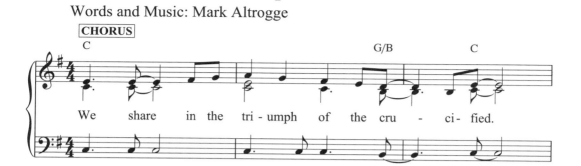

We share in the tri - umph of the cru - ci - fied.

We share in the con - quest he won.

We share in the

glo - ry of the One who died.

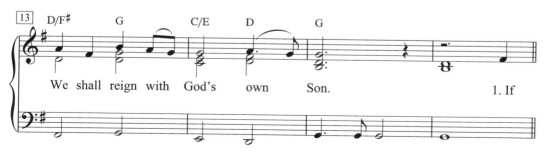

We shall reign with God's own Son. 1. If

**VERSE**

God is for us, who can be op-posed?

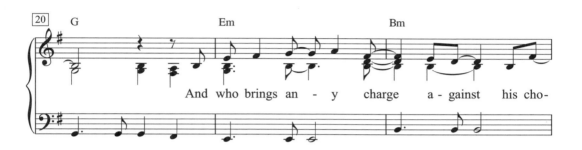

And who brings an - y charge a - gainst his cho-

- sen ones? Who con - demns

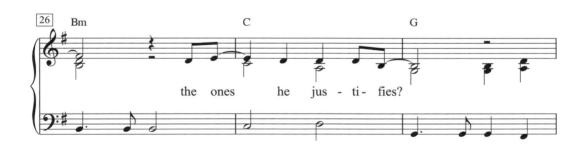

the ones he jus - ti - fies?

What can sep - a - rate us from his won -

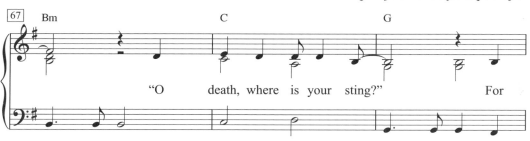

"O death, where is your sting?" For

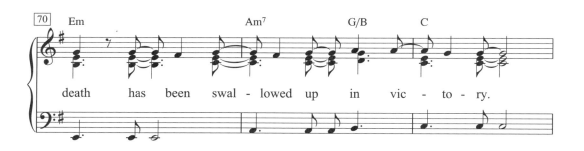

death has been swal - lowed up in vic - to - ry.

Death has been swa - lowed up in vic-

- to - ry. For

**CODA**

Son.

# Unashamed

## *You were not ashamed to be*

### Words and Music: Mark Altrogge

Gal 2:20, Gal 6:14
Php 1:20-21, Php 2:6-11
Col 1:20

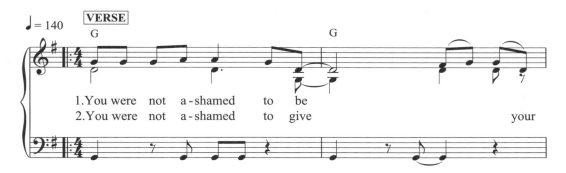

1. You were not a-shamed to be
2. You were not a-shamed to give your

emp-tied and poured out to death,
bod-y to a Ro-man lash,

un - a - shamed to give your dy-ing breath.
un - a - shamed to bear God's ho - ly wrath.

You were not a-shamed to bear
You were not a-shamed to hang

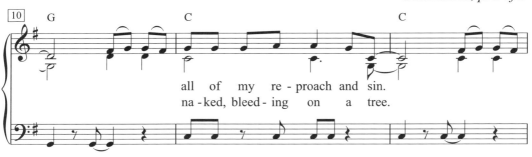

all of my re - proach and sin.
na - ked, bleed - ing on a tree.

Je - - sus, you were such a faith - ful friend.
Glad - - ly you did all of this for me.

So I will glo - ry

in the cross, and in the blood you shed for us,

glo - ry in the gos - pel of your grace. Let me be

# Undying Love

## *Grace, grace to all*

Isa 26:8, Eph 6:24
1Pe 1:6-7

Words and Music: Mark Altrogge

**VERSE**

1. Grace, grace to all who love the Lord Je-sus Christ
2. Grace, grace to all who bring the weight of their sin

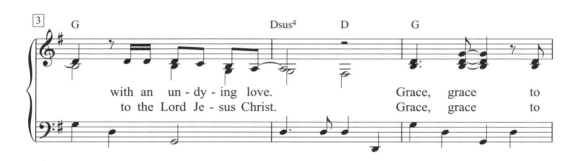

with an un-dy-ing love. Grace, grace to
to the Lord Je-sus Christ. Grace, grace to

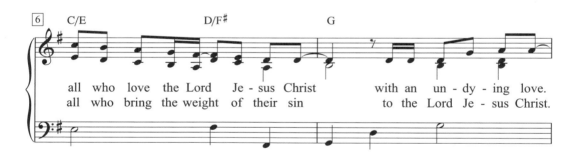

all who love the Lord Je-sus Christ with an un-dy-ing love.
all who bring the weight of their sin to the Lord Je-sus Christ.

**CHORUS**

Give me an un-dy-ing love for you, Lord, won't you set

# We Belong to You Alone
## *Creator of all*

Words and Music: Steve & Vikki Cook

Ex 19:5-6, Ex 20:4-6
1Co 6:19-20, Eph 2:19-22
Titus 2:14, 1Pe 2:4-5

1. Cre-a-tor of all, we were made for your plea-sure, you are jeal-ous for us for you see our lives as a trea-sure.
2. Al-might-y God, you've held plans for us through the a-ges, you give each life a call and a rea-son for be-ing cre-a-ted.

You want to walk with us day by day, to have a peo-ple who glad-ly say
We want to be a house you have built, a liv-ing tem-ple that you have filled.

**CHORUS**

Lord, we be-long to you a-lone.

# We Give Thanks

Ps 75:1, Rev 12:9-11

Words and Music: Mark Altrogge

# We Rejoice in the Grace of God

*He has clothed us*

Isa 61:10, Ro 5:1-2
Ro 8:17, 1Co 2:9-12
2Co 4:17, Php 3:9

Words and Music: Steve & Vikki Cook

1. He has clothed us with his right-teous-ness, cov-ered us with his great love.

He has show-ered us with mer-cy, and we de-light to know the glo-rious fa-vor, won-drous fa-vor of God.

**CHORUS**

We re-joice in the grace of God poured up-on our lives,

lov-ing kind-ness has come to us be-

cause of Je - sus Christ. We re - joice in the

grace of God, our hearts o - ver - flow.

What a joy to know the grace of God.

2. He's brought us into his family,
   made us heirs with his own Son.
   All good things he freely gives to us
   and we cannot conceive what God's preparing,
   God's preparing for us.

# We See Your Holiness

Isa 6:1-3, Isa 53:5-10
Hos 2:19, Ro 3:23-25
Jas 2:10

Words and Music: Mark Altrogge

1. We see your ho-li-ness in the pure and righ-teous laws you've made for men. We see your ho-li-ness when you move in wrath to judge and pun-ish sin. But we see your ho-li-ness most clear-ly when we see you cru-ci-fied. The

slaugh-ter of the in - no-cent to give the guilt - y life. Such se-ver-

- i - ty, such kind - ness, Lord, we thank you that you died; per - fect jus-

- tice, per - fect mer - cy side by side, per - fect jus-

- tice, per - fect mer - cy side by side.

2. We see your holiness,
   cherubim must hide their faces 'neath their wings.
   We see your holiness
   when all in heaven cast their crowns before the King.

3. We see your holiness,
   in the only blameless life this world has known.
   We see your holiness
   in your obedience to the Father's will alone.

# We Sing Your Mercies

## *Should he who made the stars*

Words and Music: Mark Altrogge

Ps 86:15, Lam 3:22
Jn 1:1-3, Ac 3:14-15
1Co 1:3

1. Should he who made the stars be hung up-on a tree?
2. Should he who is the light be cast in-to the dark?

And should the hands that healed be
And should the Lord of love be

driv - en through for me? Should he who gave us bread
pierced through his own heart? Should he who called us friends

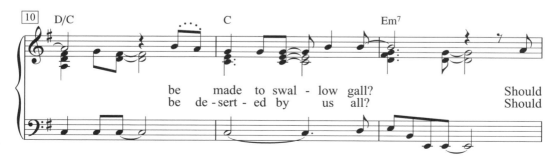

be made to swal - low gall? Should
be de - sert - ed by us all? Should

# We Trust in God

## *Our faith is not in the strength*

Words and Music: Steve & Vikki Cook

Ps 20:7-8, Ps 118:8-9
Ps 146:3-6, Jer 9:23-24
Ro 8:28-30

his love for us will en - dure. Oh,
his love for us will en - dure.

**CHORUS**

We trust in God. He's the Al - might - y One who is

sov-'reign o - ver all. We trust in God, for he's

prov - en his love and he's work - ing for our good.

We trust in God.

# We're Thirsting for You

## *Open the heavens*

Words and Music: Steve & Vikki Cook

Ps 42:1-2, Ps 63:1
Jn 4:13-15, Jn 7:37-39

# We've Been Chosen

Dt 7:6-7, 1Pe 2:9-10

Words and Music: Mark Altrogge

We've been cho - sen from all the peo - ples,

yes, we've been cho - sen to be your own.

Oh, we've been cho - sen, set a-part to be ho - ly,

to bring the glo - ry to you a - lone.

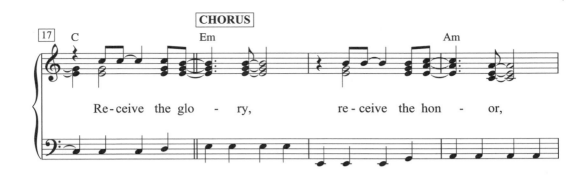

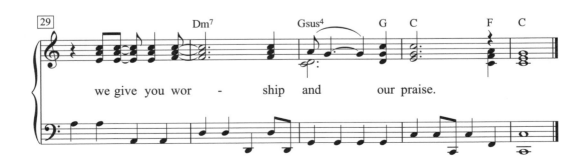

# What a Glorious Mystery

*Who can comprehend*

Words and Music: Stephen Altrogge

Job 37:5, Ps 40:5
Isa 55:8-9, 1Co 13:12
Col 1:27

# What a Hope

Eph 1:15-21, Eph 3:20-21
2Pe 1:3-4, 2Pe 3:13

Words and Music: Bob Kauflin

3. Oh, how great is your perfect might,
deliv'ring us from the darkest night.
Your holy pow'r to do what's right,
oh, how great is your perfect might.

# What Love Is This?

Jn 15:13, Ro 5:10
Gal 1:3-5, Gal 2:20

## Words and Music: Mark Altrogge

1. What love is this that came to die for me? You gave your life for all your en-e-mies, your back you of-fered free-ly to the lash. You took my guilt and bore God's ho-ly wrath. You loved

# What You Began

Ps 139:4, Ro 8:28-29
Php 1:6, Jas 1:2-4

Words and Music: Dave Fournier

CHORUS

What you be - gan you will fin - ish; by your strong

hand I will pre - vail. Ev - er - y trial you work in

it and your faith - ful - ness can't fail. Though I do

not claim to un - der - stand the mys - t'ries of your sov-

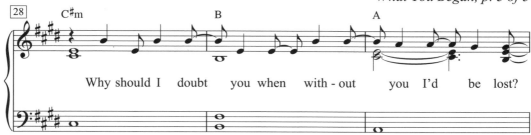

Why should I doubt you when with-out you I'd be lost?

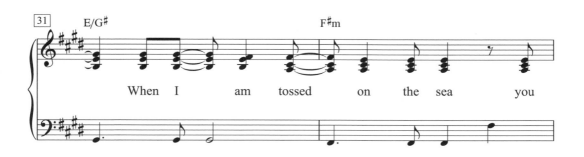

When I am tossed on the sea you

bring me back to the land

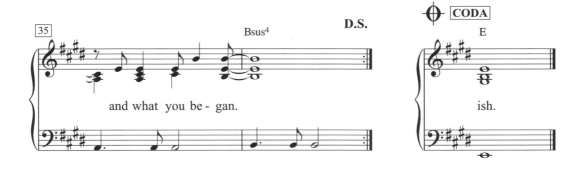

and what you be - gan.

ish.

2. You are the One who will work all things for my good,
   you are the One who guards my path before I look.
   Why should I try to walk by sight and not by faith?
   Lord, give me the grace to have
   a childlike trust in your plan
   and what you began.

# Who Is Like Our God?

## *The Lord is not our equal*

Words and Music: Eric Grover

Ex 15:11, Ps 2:1-5
Ps 33:10-11, Isa 40:12-18
Ro 11:34

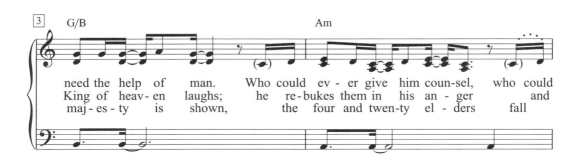

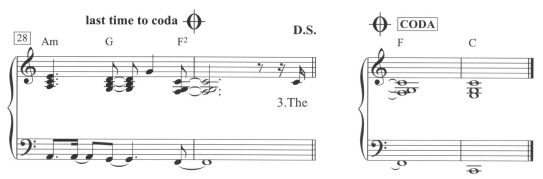

# Who Is Like You?

Ex 15:11, 2Sa 7:18-22
Ps 71:19, Isa 57:15
Lam 3:22-23

Words and Music: Mark Altrogge

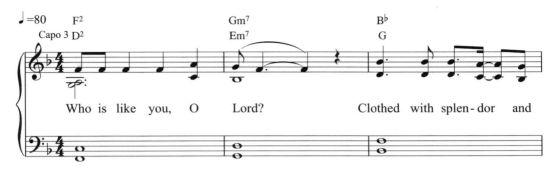

Who is like you, O Lord? Clothed with splen-dor and

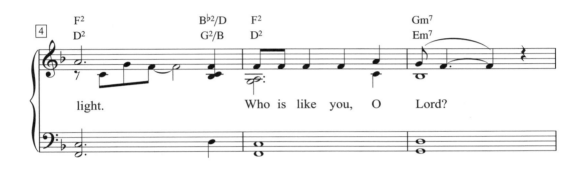

light. Who is like you, O Lord?

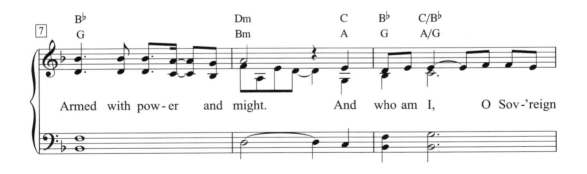

Armed with pow-er and might. And who am I, O Sov-'reign

Lord, that I should know your love? Con-

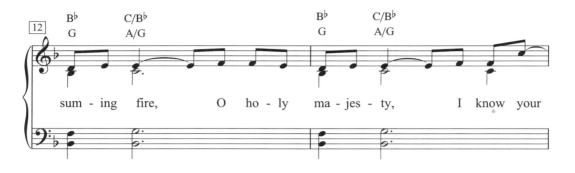

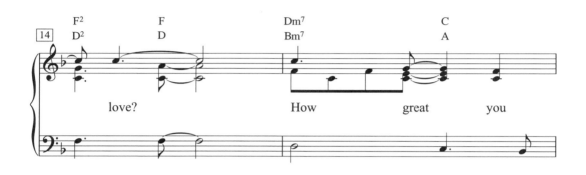

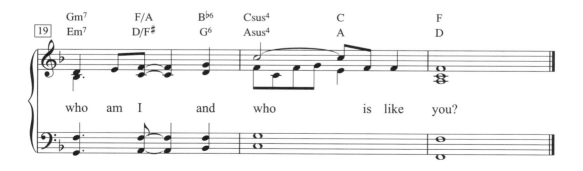

# Wonder on Wonder
## *The closer I come to you*

Words and Music: Mark Altrogge

Ps 27:4, Ps 96:6
Jn 14:6, 2Co 4:6

Lyrics:

The clos-er I come to you, the more I see all that's true, the more I find all that is ho-ly. The near-er to you I draw, the more I am filled with awe. I'm so o-ver-whelmed by your beau-ty.

**CHORUS**

Won - der on won - der, the more I look, the

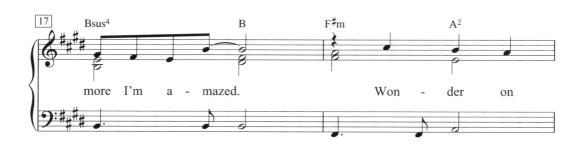

more I'm a - mazed. Won - der on

won - der, I see the glo - ry of God in your face.

In your face, I find won-

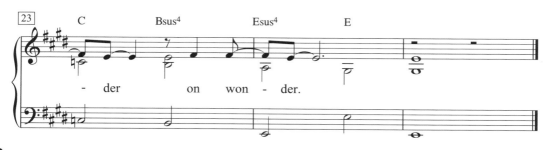

- der on won - der.

# Wonderful Savior

### *How can we not sing out*
### Words and Music: Mark Altrogge

Ps 13:6, Ps 40:9-11
Ps 71:23, Ps 108:1-4

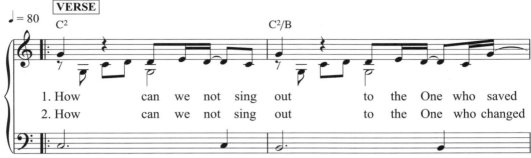

1. How can we not sing out to the One who saved
2. How can we not sing out to the One who changed

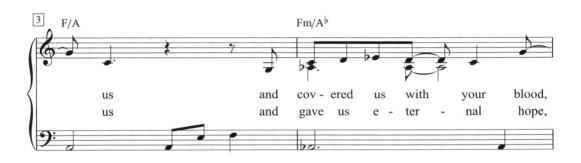

us and cov-ered us with your blood,
us and gave us e-ter-nal hope,

cast-ing all our sin in-to your sea of mer-
cap-tur-ing our hearts, flood-ing us with glad-

-cy, crown-ing us with your love?
-ness, that some-day we'll see your face?

CHORUS
9 E♭ E♭/D Cm
Won-der-ful Sav - ior, beau-ti-ful Je - sus,
12 A♭maj7 B♭ E♭
bend-ing down to lift us up out of our dark
14 E♭/D Cm A♭maj7 B♭
- ness, in-to your bright - ness, call-ing us your own.
17 F F/E Dm
Won-der-ful Sav - ior, beau-ti-ful Je - sus,
20 B♭maj7 C F
we will al-ways love you, won-der-ful Sav -
22 F/E B♭maj7 Fm/A♭ B♭ F
- ior, beau-ti-ful Je - sus.

# You Are Always with Me

*You know everything about me*

Words and Music: Mark Altrogge

Ps 139:7-12, Mt 28:20
Heb 13:5

1. You know ev-'ry-thing a-bout me. You know when I wake and sleep. You know ev-'ry-thing I'm think-ing. You know all my se-cret deeds. You know ev-ery word I say long be-fore I say it. You know ev-ery-where I go and all my ways.

2. If I flew a-way to heav-en, Je-sus, there I would find you. If I sank in-to the o-cean, Je-sus, you would be there, too. E-ven in the dark-est night to you it's bright as day. You have laid your hand on me; it's won-der-ful.

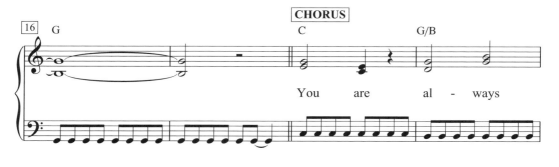

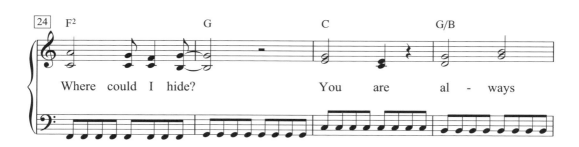

# You Are Faithful

Ro 5:1-2, 1Co 15:10
Php 2:12-13, Titus 2:11-14
1Pe 5:10

Words and Music: Mark Altrogge

2. How mighty is your grace in me
   to bring to pass your plan.
   How mighty is your grace in me,
   I will not faint but stand.
   How mighty is your grace in me,
   I will not be condemned.
   How mighty is your grace in me
   to keep me to the end.

# You Are Gentle

## *A bruised reed you will not break*

### Words and Music: Mark Altrogge

Isa 42:1-3, Isa 66:1-2
Mt 11:28-30

# You Are Greater

Ps 104:1-2, Ps 116:1-2
Ro 1:19-20, Ro 8:28
1Ti 1:17, Heb 11:3

Words and Music: Mark Altrogge

1. You are great-er than my trials, you are great-er than my fears,

you are great-er than my fail - ures, much great-er than my tears.

You cause all things to work for my good.

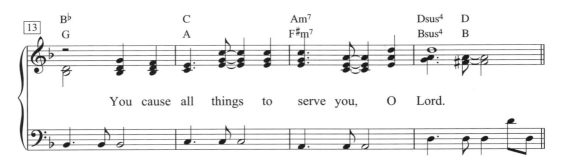

You cause all things to serve you, O Lord.

# You Are Lord

## *Once we were separated*

Words and Music: Bob Kauflin

Isa 45:22-23, Mt 28:18-20
Eph 2:12-16, Titus 3:3-7
1Pe 2:9-10, Rev 5:9-10

**CHORUS**

you, and you've brought us to-geth-er. You are Lord of

ev-'ry na-tion, you are Lord of ev-'ry tribe and race. And

by your blood we've re-ceived sal-va-tion so that we could join to-geth-er and

wor-ship you as one, and glo-ri-fy your name un-til you come.

2. Different names and faces,
   each one by your design,
   gathered from ev'ry nation,
   taken from ev'ry time
   to be a kingdom of your own,
   to serve you without end,
   and to reflect your perfect light
   to all who live in darkness and pain
   so the whole world might know that . . .

# You Are My Everything

## *I cannot thank you enough*

Ps 9:1, Ps 107:1-2
2Co 9:15, Php 3:7-8

Words and Music: Eric Hughes

1. I can-not thank you e-nough for sav-ing me;

I can-not love you e-nough for the cross;

I can-not

think e-nough a-bout you, Je - sus.

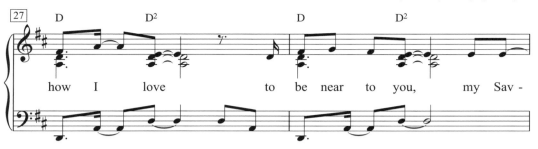

how I love to be near to you, my Sav -

- ior. Your

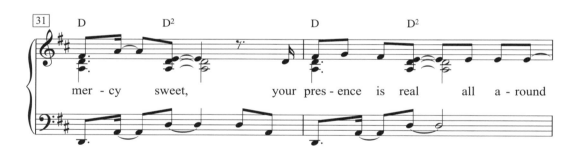

mer - cy sweet, your pres - ence is real all a - round

me, Je - sus.

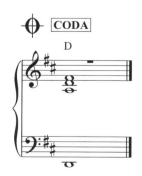

# You Are My First Love

Ps 42:1-2, Ps 73:25
Php 3:7-11

Words and Music: Steve & Vikki Cook

You are my first love, I live for you,

Lord. You're all I need and I

want noth - ing more. You are my

first love, it's you I a - dore.

You are my first love, O

# You Are My God

Ru 1:16-17

Words and Music: Mark Altrogge

# You Are the One
## *You're the One who flung the stars*

Ps 8:3-4, Ps 65:5-8
Ps 66:1-5, Ps 104:3-15
2Co 5:21

Words and Music: Mark Altrogge

1. You're the One who flung the stars a-cross the heav-ens and you are the One who spoke and moun-tains rose a - bove the foam - ing seas.

You're the One who sends the rain and gold-en sun to drench the plains, and gra-cious God, you al - ways pour such fa - vor out on me.

2. You're the One whose bleeding head was crowned with thorns,
and in my stead you took God's wrath, and died my death
that I might live your life.
And as I fix my gaze on you, I'm captivated by the view,
becoming ever like the One whose glory fills my eyes.

# You Are the Way
## *Dead in transgressions and sins*

Words and Music: Pat Sczebel

Isa 53:5, Jn 14:6
Ac 4:12, Eph 2:1-2
Php 2:8-11, Jas 1:17

1. Dead in trans-gres-sions and sins, with-out God, with-out hope in this world, then, the glo-ri-ous light of your gos-pel broke in. The Fa-ther stood up from his throne, o-pened his arms as he called out my name. Grace ir-re-sist-i-ble drew me, o-pened my eyes to see: You are the way,

# You Called Us Friends

## *You are high and lifted up*

Words and Music: Mark Altrogge

Ps 115:3, Isa 6:1-5
Isa 57:15, Jn 15:13-15

**VERSE**

1. You are high and lift-ed up, O Lord, in the most ex-alt-ed place. And the an-gels turn their eyes a-way from the splen-dor of your face. You're beau-ti-ful in ho-li-ness. You are fear-ful in your might. Yet you've o-pened up your heart to us and called us to your

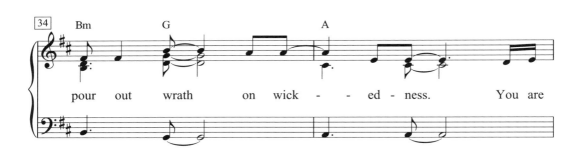

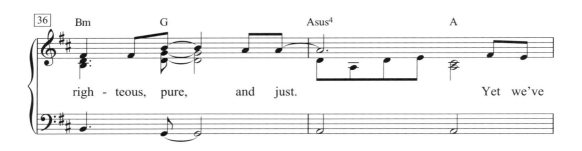

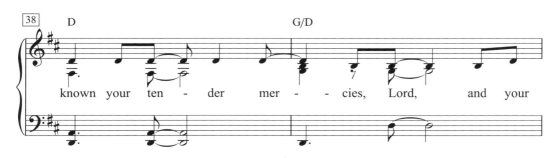

# You Have Been Given

Isa 43:7, Php 2:9-11
1Pe 2:9, Rev 5:9

Words and Music: Bob Kauflin

1. You have been giv-en the Name a-bove all names, and we

wor - - ship you, yes, we wor - - ship you.

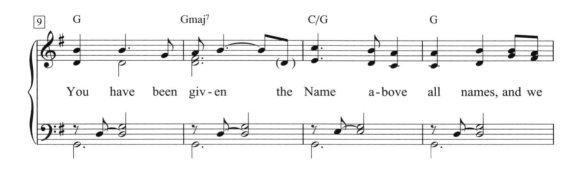

You have been giv-en the Name a-bove all names, and we

wor - - - - - - ship you, and we

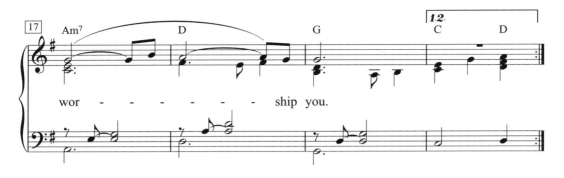

wor - - - - - - ship you.

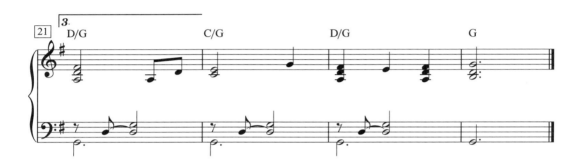

2. We are your people, made for your glory,
   and we worship you, yes, we worship you.
   We are your people, made for your glory,
   and we worship you, and we worship you.

3. You have redeemed us from ev'ry nation,
   and we worship you, yes, we worship you.
   You have redeemed us from ev'ry nation,
   and we worship you, and we worship you.

# You Have Been My Confidence

Ps 27:13-14, Ps 34:18-22
Ps 71:6-14, Ps 139:13-16
2Co 1:3-4, Heb 6:17-20

Words and Music: Mark Altrogge

# You Have Been My Confidence

Ps 27:13-14, Ps 34:18-22
Ps 71:6-14, Ps 139:13-16
2Co 1:3-4, Heb 6:17-20

Words and Music: Mark Altrogge

Gently

**VERSE**

1. You have been my con-fi-dence, O Lord, you have been my con-fi-dence, O Lord. From the womb you have sus-tained me and be-fore I knew your name, e-ven then you were my strength and my sup-port. Oh you have been my con-fi-dence, O Lord. So I will

# You Have Captured Me

*I have tasted of a love*

Words and Music: Steve & Vikki Cook

Ps 27:4, Ps 34:8
Php 3:7-8, 1Pe 1:8-9

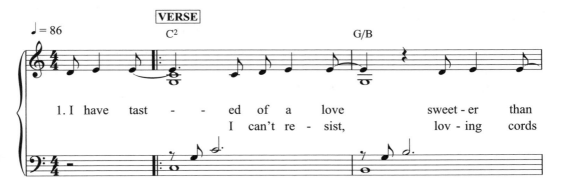

1. I have tast - - ed of a love sweet - er than
I can't re - sist, lov - ing cords

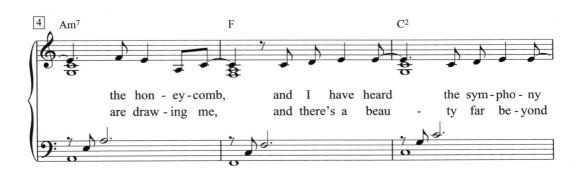

the hon - ey - comb, and I have heard the sym - pho - ny
are draw - ing me, and there's a beau - ty far be - yond

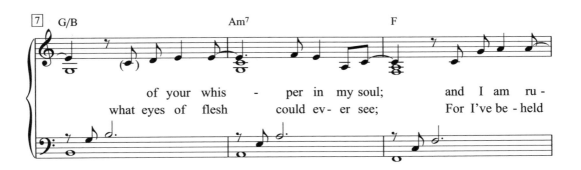

of your whis - per in my soul; and I am ru -
what eyes of flesh could ev - er see; For I've be - held

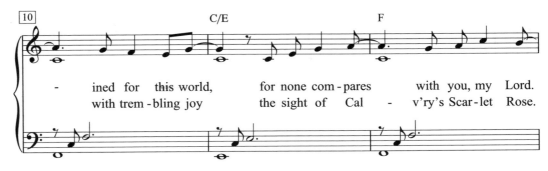

- ined for this world, for none com - pares with you, my Lord.
with trem - bling joy the sight of Cal - v'ry's Scar - let Rose.

**CHORUS**

For you have cap - - - tured me, com - plete - ly cap-

- - - tured me, and I'm con - sumed with you

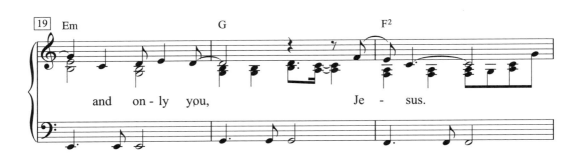

and on - ly you, Je - sus.

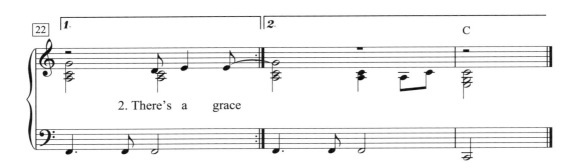

2. There's a grace

# You Have Exalted

Ps 40:17, Ps 138
Php 2:9

Words and Music: Bob Kauflin

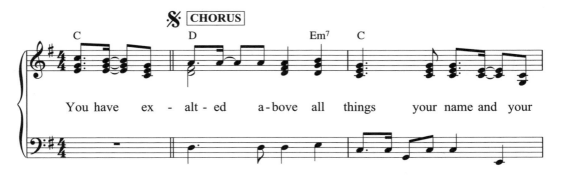

You have ex-alt-ed a-bove all things your name and your

Word. You will be faith-ful to all you've

said, your prom-ise is sure. You gave me

strength and songs to sing, you will de-liv-er me a-gain

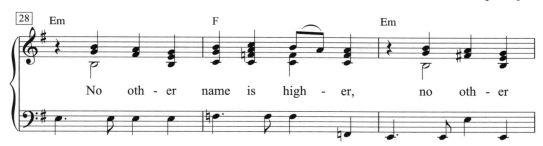

No oth-er name is high-er, no oth-er

name is good. Your name a - lone de - serves the

glo - ry for - ev - er - more.

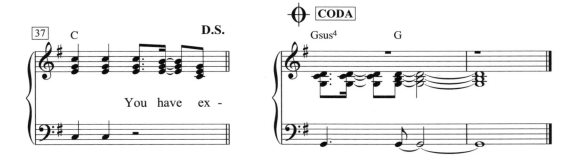

You have ex -

2. Though you are lofty and high
you keep the lowly in your sight.
Troubles may seek and find me;
your Word will still prevail
through ev'ry trial I encounter
your Word never fails.

# You Have the Power

1Ch 29:10-13, 2Ch 20:5-6
Ps 21:13, Ps 31:3-5
Ps 68:34-35, Isa 40:26

Words and Music: Mark Altrogge

**CHORUS**

You have the pow-er, O Lord.

You have the pow-er, O Lord to change

ev-'ry sit-u-a-tion, to de-liv-er from temp-ta-

-tion, to hum-ble hearts and na-tions. You have the

pow-er, you have the pow-er.

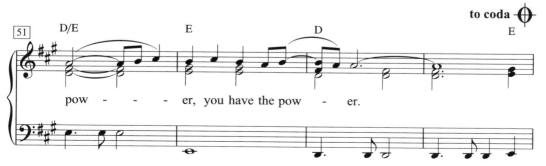

# You Heavens Adore Him

*Praise the Lord*

Verse words: anonymous, ca. 1801
Chorus words: Bob Kauflin
Music: Bob Kauflin and John Spiro

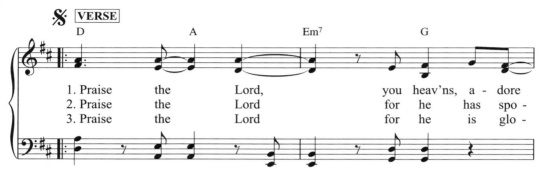

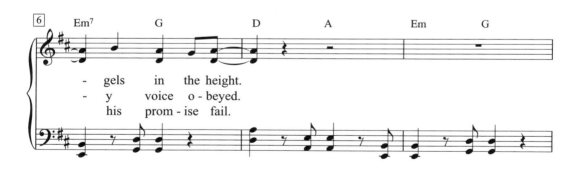

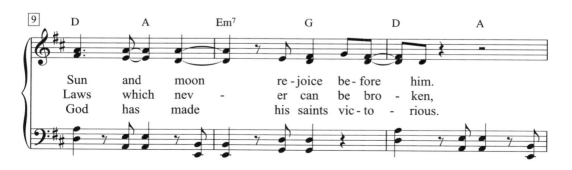

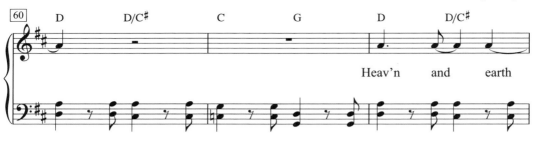

Heav'n and earth

and all cre - a - tion

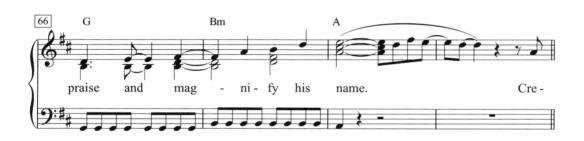

praise and mag - ni - fy his name. Cre -

**CHORUS**

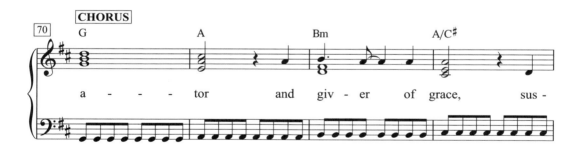

a - tor and giv - er of grace, sus -

tain - er of in - fants and kings, our

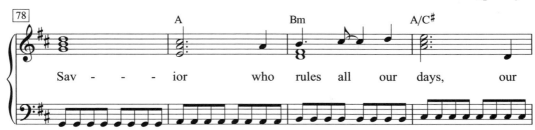

Sav - - - ior who rules all our days, our

hearts and our voic - es we bring

to praise the Lord.

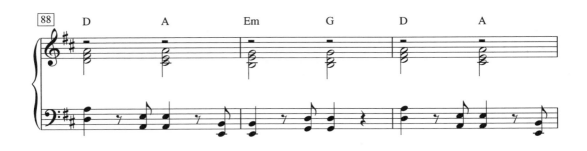

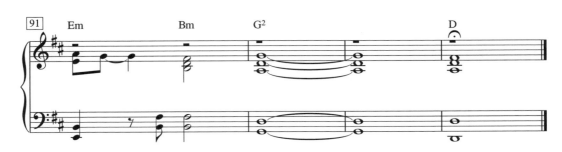

# You Left Your Glory

Ps 118:21-22, Isa 49:16
Php 2:5-9, 1Pe 2:6-7

Words and Music: Mark Altrogge

Lyrics:

You left your glo-ry for a cross to bear our guilt and car-ry our sin, and now the gates of righ-teous-ness are o-pen wide and we have come in. The stone the build-ers cast a-way, the one re-ject-ed, mocked and de-spised has now be-come the cor-ner-stone, the foun-da-tion of our lives.

# You Sat Down

Heb 1:1-4, Heb 8:1-2
Heb 10:12-13, Rev 19:11

Words and Music: Mark Altrogge

You sat down at the right hand of the Father in majesty. You sat down at the right hand of the Father in majesty. You are crowned Lord of all, you are faithful and righteous and true. You're my master, you're my owner, and I love serving you.

# You'll Never Leave Me

Ro 8:35-39, 2Co 4:16-18
Heb 4:16, Heb 12:1-2
Heb 13:5

Words and Music: Mark Altrogge

**CHORUS**

leave me, nor for - sake me. What can

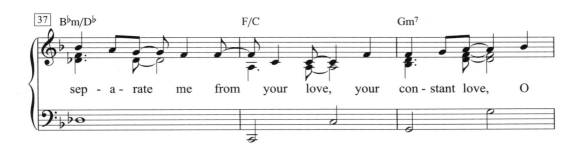

sep - a - rate me from your love, your con - stant love, O

Lord. You'll nev - er leave me,

nor for sake me. What can sep - a - rate me from

to coda

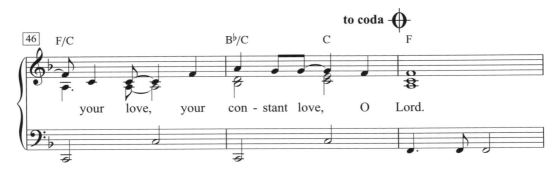

your love, your con - stant love, O Lord.

# Your Beauty and Your Majesty

Dt 30:6, Pr 16:16
1Co 15:3-4, 1Jn 4:10

Words and Music: JonRyan

# Your Great Name We Praise

## *Immortal, invisible God*

Ps 36:5-6, Ps 90:1-3
Dan 7:9, 1Ti 1:17
1Ti 6:13-16, Jas 1:17

Words: Walter Chalmers Smith
1867 Original melody traditional Welsh hymn
Alt. and new words and music: Bob Kauflin

1. Im-mor-tal, in-vis-i-ble God, on-ly wise, in
rest-ing, un-hast-ing and si-lent as light, not

light in-ac-ces-si-ble, hid from our eyes. Most
want-ing or wast-ing, you rule us in might. Your

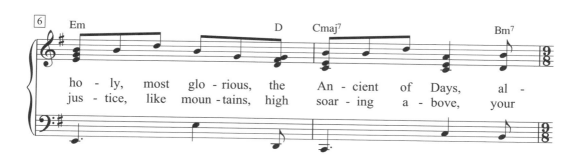

ho-ly, most glo-rious, the An-cient of Days, al-
jus-tice, like moun-tains, high soar-ing a-bove, your

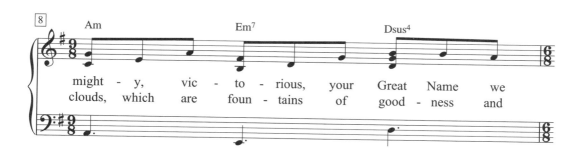

might-y, vic-to-rious, your Great Name we
clouds, which are foun-tains of good-ness and

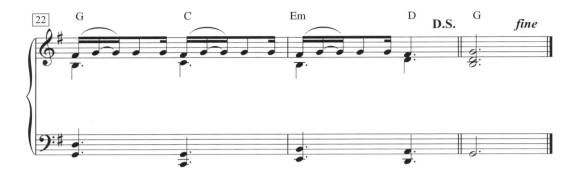

3. All life comes from you, Lord,
   to both great and small.
   In all life you live, Lord,
   the true life of all.
   We blossom and flourish,
   but quickly grow frail.
   We wither and perish,
   but you never fail.

4. Great Father of glory,
   pure Father of light,
   your angels adore you,
   all veiling their sight.
   All praise we will render,
   oh Father of grace,
   till one day in splendor
   we see face to face.

# Your Great Renown

## *Our hearts are longing*

Words: Eric Grover
Music: Eric Grover and Steve Cook

1Ch 16:31, Ps 46:10
Isa 26:8, Mt 6:10
2Co 4:7, Col 1:27

1. Our hearts are long-ing for the glo-ry of the Lord
to be made known in all the earth.
Lord, let your king-dom come; Lord, let your will be done;
yours is the great-est name of all.

**CHORUS**

We want to see the na-tions bow; We want to hear the ris-ing sound

2. Our hearts are longing for the wisdom of the Lord
   to be proclaimed in all the earth.
   Your ways are higher than the dreams of any man;
   yours is the greatest name of all.

3. Our hearts are hungry for the power of the Lord
   to be displayed in all the earth.
   The message of the cross will bring hope to the lost;
   yours is the greatest name of all.

# Your Great Salvation

*You knew us each by name*

Words and Music: Steve & Vikki Cook

Dt 33:26-27, Ps 33:8-11
Isa 26:3-4, Ro 8:28-32
1Co 15:51-52, Eph 1:3-6

1. You knew us each by name be-fore the
2. You free-ly gave your Son to buy our

dawn of time.
righ - teous-ness.

You chose us as your own, this was your
So we could be con - formed un - to your

heart's de - light.
ho - li - ness.

To re - veal your glo - ry you have
One day we'll be changed and see you

There is no pow-er that can hold back your hand from

do - ing all you've planned. And

we stand se - cure up - on your great sal - va -

**TURN**

tion.

# Your Hand Upon Me

### *O Lord, you have searched me*

Ps 139:1-10

Words and Music: Eric Grover

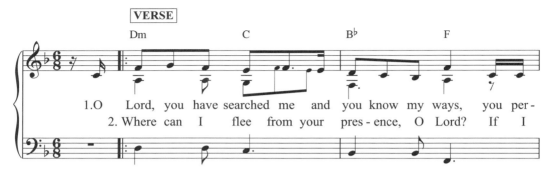

**VERSE**

1.O Lord, you have searched me and you know my ways, you per-
2. Where can I flee from your pres-ence, O Lord? If I

ceive all my thoughts from a-far. Your
sleep in the depths you are there. Your

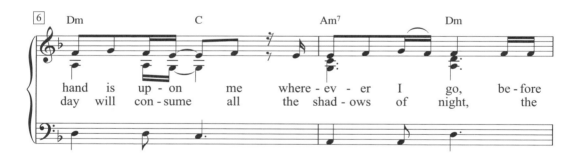

hand is up-on me where-ev-er I go, be-fore
day will con-sume all the shad-ows of night, the

I form a word you al-read-y know.
dark can-not hide from your bril-liant light.

# Your Holiness Is Beautiful

*How wondrous is your presence*

Words and Music: Mark Altrogge

Ps 27:4, Ps 29:2
1Co 13:12, 2Co 3:18
2Co 4:6

2. I long to see your splendor, Lord,
   you've burned it in my heart.
   My hunger won't be satisfied
   to worship from afar.
   Oh cause your face to shine on me
   and take the veil away.
   And then my joy will be complete,
   I'll sing eternal praise.

# Your Holy Majesty

## *You are high above all things*

Words and Music: Mark Altrogge

Isa 61:10, Gal 3:13
Heb 1:3, 1Jn 4:10
Jude 25

1. You are high a-bove all things, the heav-ens can't con-
2. Why would you shed your own blood for those who spurned your

tain your ra-diance and your beau - - ty.
love and so man - y times re - fused your grace?

You shine bright-er than the sun, I'm rav-ished and un -
Why would you take up our curse, why did you love us

done, you've con-quered me com - plete - ly. Now
first? Oh you de-serve e - ter - nal praise.

I am long-ing for the time when I will see your

**CHORUS**

ho - ly, ho - ly maj - es - ty, your

glo - ry and your splen - dor. Ho - ly, ho - ly

maj - es - ty, you fill my soul with won - der and un-

speak - a - ble de-light at just the sight of your

ho - ly maj - es - ty.

# Your Kingdom Is Glorious
## *You have ascended*

Words and Music: Steve & Vikki Cook

Ps 145:10-13, Ps 146:10
1Ti 1:17, Heb 1:8-12
Rev 11:15

1. You have as-cend-ed and tak-en your throne.
2. You rule with kind-ness o-ver the land.

All this world's king-doms
Peace and pro-vi-sion

will be your own. For yours is all
come from your hand. And we crown you Cre-

wis-dom. Yours is all pow-er.
a-tor. We crown you, O Sav-ior.

Yours is all hon-or and strength. Your
We crown you most high, King of Kings.

# Your Love

Ps 36:5-8, Jer 31:3
Ro 8:29, Heb 12:6
1Jn 4:10, Rev 22:1-2

Words and Music: Bob Kauflin

# Your Love for Me

## *Sometimes I don't get everything*

1Ch 17:16-17, Ps 73:25-26
1Ti 6:6

Words and Music: Mark Altrogge

1. Some-times I don't get ev-'ry-thing I ask, some-
   times my hand grows wear-y at the task, oh

times I e-ven find my-self in need. But
fan a-gain the flame that grows so weak. Re-

oh, it is so good to know that you're al-ways near to
mind me of the glo-ries of my fu-ture in you, of

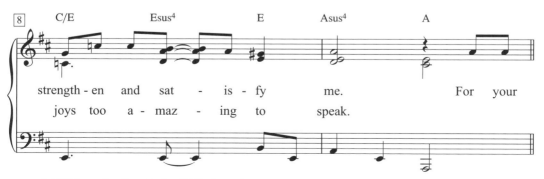

strength-en and sat-is-fy me. For your
joys too a-maz-ing to speak.

# Your Love Is Higher
## *When I'm weak*

Ps 61:4, Mt 12:20-21
Ro 8:35-39, Eph 3:18-19
Jude 24-25

### Words and Music: Mark Altrogge

1. When I'm

**VERSE**

weak    and when I fail,    the
strong    and pros-per-ing,    I'll

pow-er of your might-y cross pre-vails.    When I'm
prize your love a-bove all oth-er things.    So I re-

tried    and when I'm pressed    in the
joice    I will de-light    that my

shel - ter of your wings I find my rest,
name is writ - ten in your book of life,
O
O

**CHORUS**

Lord.
Lord.
Your love is high - er than the heights,

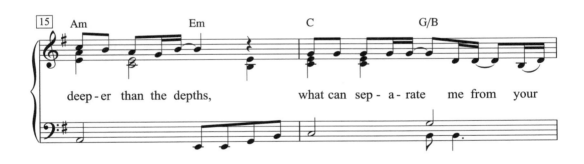

deep - er than the depths, what can sep - a - rate me from your

love? Your love is long - er than this life,

strong - er than death.     Je - sus, you will keep me in    your   love,

Je - sus, you will keep    me in     your     love.

2. When I'm    love.

# Your Love Stands Firm

Ps 119:89-90, Isa 49:15-16
Ro 8:1-2, Eph 2:4-7

Words and Music: Mark Altrogge

**CHORUS**

Your love stands firm in the heav - ens. You loved us be - fore time be - gan. From age to age you will show us your love. You've en - graved us up - on your hands. Your hands.

**VERSE**

1. Through - out e - ter - ni - ty we'll mar - vel at your

# Your Mercy and Kindness

## *O Lord, you are my shepherd*

Ps 23

Words and Music: Mark Altrogge

# Your Own Love

## *I want to love your son*

Words and Music: Mark Altrogge

Jn 3:35, Jn 17:24
Php 2:8-11

# Your Praise Will Never Cease

*There's an ancient song*

Words: Steve Cook and Bob Kauflin
Music: Steve Cook

Ps 93:1-2, Lam 5:19
Rev 4:9-11, Rev 5:13

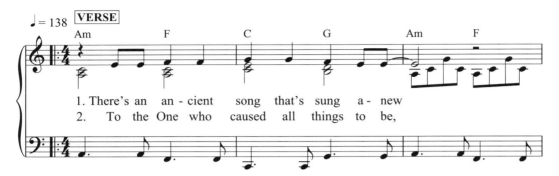

1. There's an an-cient song that's sung a-new
2. To the One who caused all things to be,

by the ones who live to wor-ship you;
to the One who rules in sov-'reign-ty,

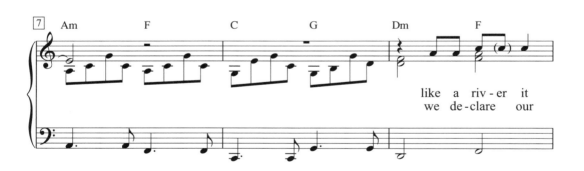

like a riv-er it
we de-clare our

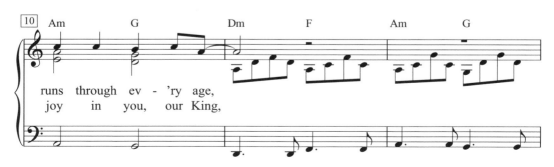

runs through ev-'ry age,
joy in you, our King,

**13** driv-en by the glo-ry of your grace.
and de-light in be-ing your re-deemed.

**CHORUS**

**16** And when we've sung your praise for a thou-sand years we'll have

**19** just be-gun to sing, for your throne will reign through e-

**22** ter-ni-ty and your praise will nev-er cease, it will nev-er cease.

# Your Redeeming Love

## *I come boldly*

Words and Music: Mark Altrogge

Ps 63:1-2, 1Co 1:18-19
Gal 6:14, Php 3:3
Heb 4:16, Heb 10:19-22

I come bold - ly, trust - ing on - ly your re - deem - ing love,

flow - ing free - ly from your side now,

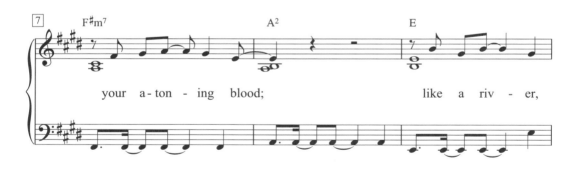

your a - ton - ing blood; like a riv - er,

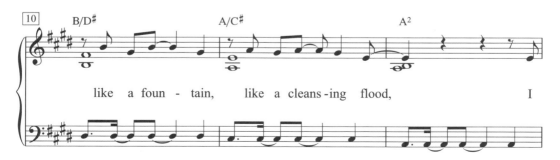

like a foun - tain, like a cleans - ing flood, I

# Your Sovereign Grace

*There are strong arms*

### Words and Music: Steve & Vikki Cook

Ps 16:5-11, Eph 1:11-12
Eph 2:8-9, Heb 6:19-20

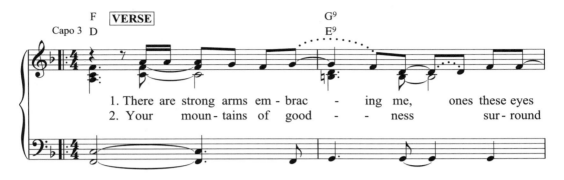

1. There are strong arms em-brac - ing me, ones these eyes
2. Your moun-tains of good - - ness sur - round

of flesh can - not see
me and reach to the sky

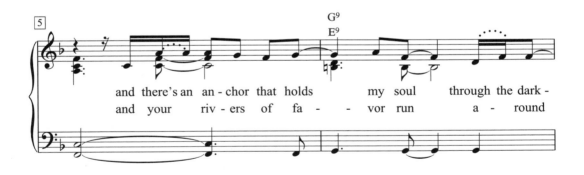

and there's an an - chor that holds my soul through the dark -
and your riv - ers of fa - - vor run a - round

- est rag - ing sea. For you said that
me on ev - 'ry side. For I know that

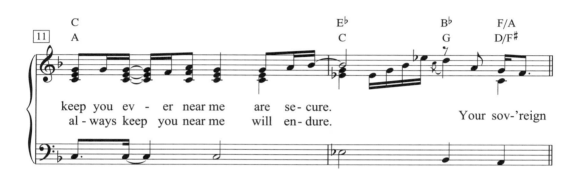

**CHORUS**

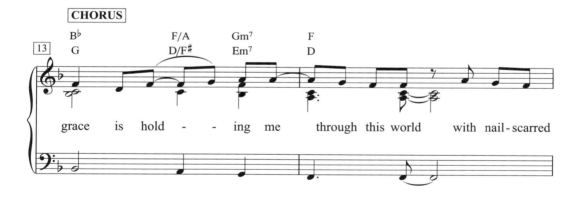

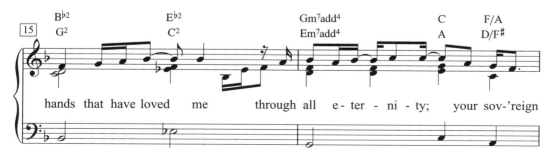

grace is hold - ing me through this world. I rest

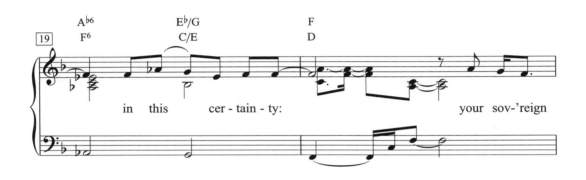

in this cer - tain - ty: your sov-'reign

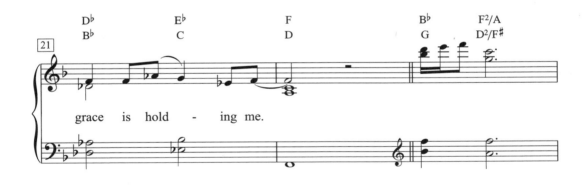

grace is hold - ing me.

# Your Word, O Lord

Ps 119:11, 1Th 2:13
Heb 4:12, 2Pe 1:3-4

Words and Music: Bob Kauflin

Your word, O Lord, is liv-ing, is liv-

-ing and ac-tive. Your word, O Lord, is work-

-ing in me. Your prom-is-es

are sure. Your faith-ful-ness en-dures.

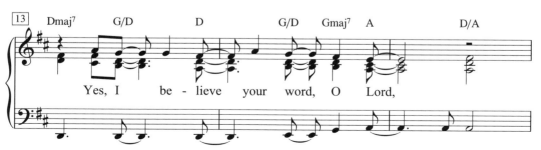

Yes, I be-lieve your word, O Lord,

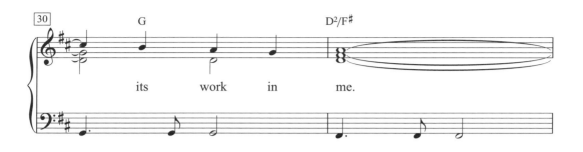

its work in me.

Lord, you know I tru -

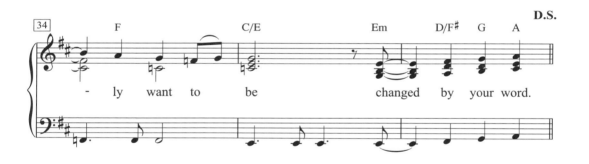

- ly want to be changed by your word.

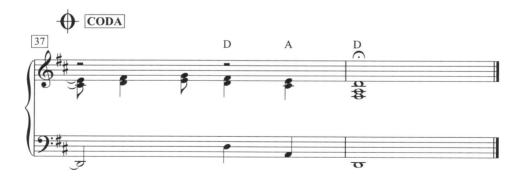

# You're So Good to Me
## *You've given me so much*

Ps 13:5-6, Ps 103:10-11
Heb 13:5, Jas 1:17
Rev 22:4

### Words and Music: Steve & Vikki Cook

1. You've giv-en me so much more than I'd ev-er dreamed and so much more than I de-serve. Your mer-cies sur-round me, re-mind-ing me a-new that all I have has come from you, it's all from you.

For you have crowned my days with o-ver-whelm-

- ing grace, Lord, you're so good to me.

Though trou - bles fall like rain, this pre - cious truth

re - mains, Lord, you're so good to me,

yes, you're so good to me.

2. You chose me, you saved me
   and made me your own;
   promised that you would never leave.
   Soon one day, you'll call me
   and we'll see face to face,
   'til then you've given me a taste of paradise.

# You've Captured My Heart

## *You gently pursued me*

Words and Music: Steve & Vikki Cook

Ps 63:1-3, Ps 84:10-12
Ps 145:5, Ro 2:4

1. You gently pursued me. Lord, how I love you. You tenderly drew me. Lord, how I love you. Your grace over-flowing poured on me like a flood. And you over-whelmed me with your conquering

long for you only. Lord, how I love you. To gaze on your glory, Lord, how I love you. How awesome your spendor, what great beauty and light, unspeakable holiness and infinite

# A NOTE
# TO GUITARISTS

We offer here common fingering options for some of the chords found in this songbook. But we also recommend you use your favorite complete chord book. It can help you learn each song accurately and comfortably by identifying fingerings that fit your playing style and skill level. Websites such as www.chordfind.com can also be helpful.

# GUITAR CHORDS

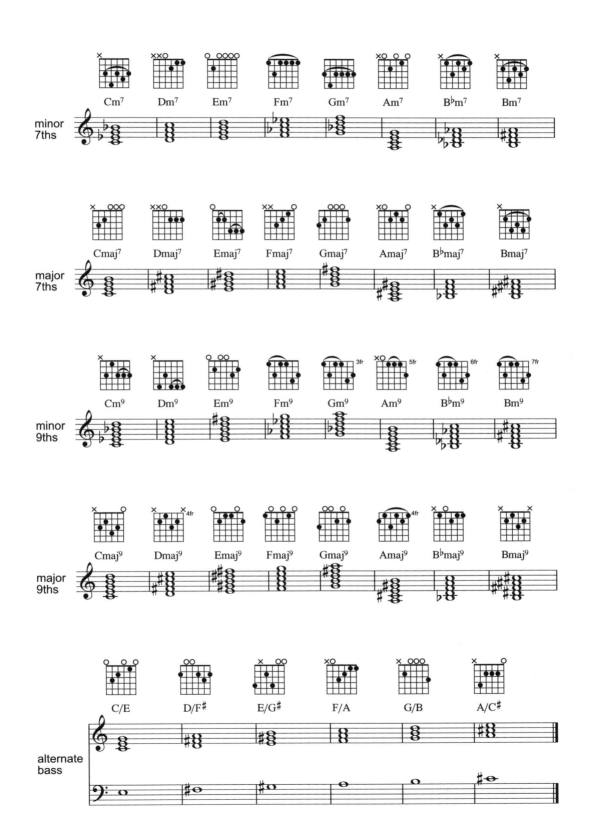

# SONG INDEX

*CD Key appears following this Song Index

| SONG TITLE | VOL 1 | VOL 2 | CD | SONG TITLE | VOL 1 | VOL 2 | CD |
|---|---|---|---|---|---|---|---|
| *Holy God, in love, became* | – | 138 | 12,13 | *Jesus, how we love you* | – | 131 | 4 |
| **Holy Love** | 204 | – | – | *Jesus, I love you* | 109 | – | – |
| **Holy Spirit, Move Among Us** | 206 | – | – | **Jesus, King and Conqueror** | 296 | – | – |
| **Holy, Holy Are You Lord** | 211 | – | – | **Jesus, Light of the Nations** | 298 | – | – |
| **Hope of Glory (The)** | – | **142** | – | **Jesus, My Only Hope** | 301 | – | 9 |
| *How can I ever begin* | 187 | – | 8 | **Jesus, Thank You** | 303 | – | 14 |
| *How can we not sing out* | – | 223 | 12 | **Jesus, You Reign over All** | 307 | – | – |
| **How Close** | 214 | – | – | **Join All the Glorious Names** | 309 | – | 7 |
| *How do I know you love me?* | 243 | – | 1 | **King of Grace** | 311 | – | 7 |
| *How do I thank you, O Lord* | 43 | – | 5,10 | **Know You** | 313 | – | 8 |
| *How do you love me?* | – | 3 | – | **Let All That Is Within Me** | – | 1 | – |
| **How Excellent Is Your Name** | 217 | – | – | **Let Me Count the Ways** | – | 3 | – |
| **How Firm a Foundation** | 221 | – | 6 | **Let Praise Ascend** | – | 5 | – |
| **How Great You Are** | 223 | – | – | **Let the Name of Jesus** | – | 7 | – |
| **How High and How Wide** | 226 | – | 10 | **Let Us Draw Near** | – | 10 | – |
| *How lovely you are* | – | 147 | – | **Let Your Joy Come Down** | – | 14 | – |
| **How Majestic** | 228 | – | 14 | **Lift Up Your Eyes** | – | 17 | 9 |
| **How Wonderful Your Love** | 231 | – | – | **Like a River Glorious** | – | 19 | 11 |
| *How wondrous is your presence* | – | 290 | 5 | *Long ago* | – | 111 | 8 |
| **I Bow Down** | 234 | – | 6 | **Look (The)** | – | 144 | 11 |
| *I cannot thank you enough* | – | 236 | 7 | *Look upon this fearful scene* | 92 | – | 14 |
| *I come boldly* | – | 312 | 7 | **Lord Jesus, Come** | – | 22 | 5 |
| **I Come by the Blood** | 237 | – | 12 | **Lord of the Harvest** | – | 24 | – |
| *I come into your presence* | 301 | – | 9 | *Lord, by your grace we stand* | 61 | – | – |
| *I do not seek* | – | 176 | – | *Lord, change my heart* | – | 39 | – |
| *I don't deserve* | 37 | – | 14 | **Lord, I Live by Your Word** | – | 27 | – |
| *I drink deep from your well* | 249 | – | 6 | *Lord, I'll count it all joy* | 81 | – | 14 |
| *I have found my treasure* | – | 55 | – | *Lord, there is no one like you* | – | 22 | 5 |
| *I have one passion* | – | 125 | 9 | *Lord, what moved your heart* | – | 166 | 6,12 |
| **I Have Seen with My Eyes** | 239 | – | – | *Lord, you're calling me to come* | – | 128 | 12 |
| *I have tasted of a love* | – | 255 | 7 | **Love of a Holy God (The)** | – | **147** | – |
| **I Long for You, O Lord** | 241 | – | – | **Make His Praise Great** | – | 29 | 10 |
| **I Look to the Cross** | 243 | – | 1 | *Make us a people of your presence* | 3 | – | – |
| **I Look Up** | 245 | – | 3 | *Man of sorrows, what a name* | 169 | – | 11 |
| **I Love the Cross** | 247 | – | 6 | **May Thy Kingdom Come** | – | 31 | – |
| *I love you, Lord* | – | 1 | – | **Mercies Anew** | – | 33 | 11 |
| **I Must Have You** | 249 | – | 6 | **Mighty God** | – | 35 | – |
| *I once was a slave to sin* | 135 | – | – | **Mighty, Mighty Savior** | – | 37 | 13 |
| *I saw one hanging on a tree* | – | 144 | 11 | **More and More Like You** | – | 39 | – |
| **I Stand in Awe** | 252 | – | 10 | **More of You** | – | 40 | – |
| *I want to love your son* | – | 308 | – | *More of you and less of me* | – | 40 | – |
| **I Want to Tell You** | 254 | – | – | **More Than Life Itself** | – | 43 | 6 |
| **I Will Boast in the Cross** | 256 | – | 3 | *Most Holy Judge* | 274 | – | – |
| **I Will Fix My Eyes** | 259 | – | – | **Most Wonderful of All (The)** | – | **149** | – |
| *I will give thanks* | – | 68 | 10 | *My defender, my hope* | 285 | – | – |
| **I Will Glory in My Redeemer** | 262 | – | 8,11,12 | **My Father** | – | 45 | – |
| *I will praise you all my life* | – | 59 | 10 | *My Father, how you care for me* | – | 157 | – |
| *I will rejoice in you* | 185 | – | – | **My Glorious Hope** | – | 48 | 9 |
| **I Will Wait** | 264 | – | – | **My Glory and the One Who Lifts My Head** | – | 51 | – |
| **If You Are for Us** | 266 | – | – | *My hope is not in this life* | 39 | – | – |
| **I'm Calling Out** | 270 | – | 6 | *My Savior's sacrifice* | 50 | – | 12 |
| **I'm Forever Grateful** | 272 | – | – | *My soul finds rest in you alone* | – | 43 | 6 |
| *I'm gonna trust in God* | 149 | – | 4 | *Never has a death* | – | 154 | – |
| **I'm Justified** | 274 | – | – | *No eye has seen* | 226 | – | 10 |
| *Immortal, invisible God* | – | 280 | 11 | **No God but God** | – | 53 | – |
| **In My Heart** | 276 | – | 7 | *No one is good* | – | 37 | 13 |
| **In the Presence** | 278 | – | 10 | **No Sacrifice** | – | 55 | – |
| **In View of Your Mercy** | 280 | – | – | *Not to us* | – | 97 | 14 |
| **In You Alone** | 283 | – | 7 | **Not to Us** | – | 57 | – |
| **In Your Shadow** | 285 | – | – | **O Faithful God** | – | 59 | 10 |
| **Isn't He Good** | 287 | – | 14 | **O Give Thanks** | – | 61 | – |
| **It Should Have Been Me** | 290 | – | 2 | **O God, My God** | – | 63 | – |
| **It's All for You** | 292 | – | 2 | **O God, Our Help in Ages Past** | – | 65 | 14 |
| **Jesus Came to Earth** | 294 | – | 13 | *O God, our Redeemer* | 98 | – | 6 |
| *Jesus, friend of sinners* | 201 | – | 14 | | | | |

| SONG TITLE | VOL 1 | VOL 2 | CD |
|---|---|---|---|
| O God, there's none like you | 127 | – | 13 |
| O God, you see the times | 223 | – | – |
| O Lord, our Lord | 217 | – | – |
| O Lord, you are my shepherd | – | 306 | 8 |
| O Lord, you have searched me | – | 288 | 8 |
| **O Most High** | – | **68** | **10** |
| **O Wondrous Love** | – | **70** | **8** |
| Oh gather around the throne | 103 | – | 9 |
| Oh the depths of your riches | 138 | – | – |
| **Once This Heart** | – | **73** | – |
| Once we had not received | 78 | – | – |
| Once we were dead in transgressions | 15 | – | – |
| Once we were separated | – | 234 | 10 |
| **One and Only God (The)** | – | **151** | **3** |
| **One Pure and Holy Passion** | – | **76** | – |
| **Only in the Cross** | – | **78** | **12** |
| **Only You for Me** | – | **81** | **1** |
| **Open Our Eyes** | – | **83** | – |
| Open the heavens | – | 202 | – |
| Our faith is not in the strength | – | 200 | – |
| Our hearts are longing | – | 283 | 7 |
| **Perfect Lamb of God** | – | **87** | **14** |
| **Pleasing in Your Sight** | – | **90** | – |
| **Power and the Glory (The)** | – | **154** | – |
| **Praise God** | – | **92** | **11** |
| Praise the Lord | – | 264 | 11 |
| **Prize of My Life (The)** | – | **157** | – |
| **Raise Up an Army** | – | **95** | – |
| **Receive the Glory** | – | **97** | **14** |
| **Rock of Ages, Cleft for Me** | – | **99** | **11** |
| Should he who made the stars | – | 198 | 2,10 |
| **Shout** | – | **100** | **5** |
| **Show Me Your Glory** | – | **104** | – |
| **Showers of Mercy** | – | **106** | **4** |
| Soaring mountains | – | 149 | – |
| **Soli Deo Gloria** | – | **108** | **9** |
| Sometimes I don't get everything | – | 298 | 4 |
| **Song of the Lamb** | – | **111** | **8** |
| Sovereign Creator | 307 | – | – |
| Sovereign God | – | 51 | – |
| **Sovereign One** | – | **113** | **13** |
| Spirit, how we hunger | 117 | – | 1 |
| **Surrender All** | – | **116** | **14** |
| Take all I am, Lord | – | 116 | 14 |
| Thank you for the cross | 182 | – | 4,10 |
| **Thank You for the Cross** | – | **118** | – |
| Thank you, Lord | – | 142 | – |
| **That I Might Gain Christ** | – | **120** | **5** |
| **The Almighty God Is with Me** | – | **123** | – |
| **The Audience of One** | – | **125** | **9** |
| The closer I come to you | – | 221 | – |
| **The Glories of Calvary** | – | **128** | **12** |
| **The Glory of the Ages** | – | **131** | **4** |
| **The Glory of the Cross** | – | **134** | **7,12** |
| **The Glory of the Lamb** | – | **136** | **9** |
| **The Gospel Song** | – | **138** | **12,13** |
| **The Highest Glory** | – | **140** | **10** |
| **The Hope of Glory** | – | **142** | – |
| The light of day | – | 87 | 14 |
| **The Look** | – | **144** | **11** |
| The Lord is good and does good | 23 | – | – |
| The Lord is not our equal | – | 216 | 8 |
| **The Love of a Holy God** | – | **147** | – |
| **The Most Wonderful of All** | – | **149** | – |

| SONG TITLE | VOL 1 | VOL 2 | CD |
|---|---|---|---|
| The mystery of the cross | 303 | – | 14 |
| **The One and Only God** | – | **151** | **3** |
| **The Power and the Glory** | – | **154** | – |
| **The Prize of My Life** | – | **157** | – |
| The wonder of your mercy | 85 | – | 4 |
| **Then Your Grace Appeared** | – | **159** | – |
| There are strong arms | – | 315 | 4 |
| There is joy in heaven | – | 14 | – |
| There is no more separation | 10 | – | 8 |
| **There Is No One Like Our God** | – | **161** | – |
| **There Is One Thing** | – | **164** | – |
| There's an ancient song | – | 310 | 7 |
| **This Fathomless Love** | – | **166** | **6,12** |
| **This I Know** | – | **169** | – |
| This storm-tossed heart | 283 | – | 7 |
| **Those Who Know Their God** | – | **172** | – |
| Though the earth should tremble | 96 | – | – |
| Though the mountains fall | – | 123 | – |
| Though waves of troubles come | – | 48 | 9 |
| **Three in One** | – | **174** | **13** |
| To all earthly beauty | 34 | – | – |
| **To Be with You** | – | **176** | – |
| **Treasured Possession** | – | **178** | – |
| **Triumph of the Crucified** | – | **180** | – |
| **Unashamed** | – | **185** | **9** |
| **Undying Love** | – | **188** | – |
| **We Belong to You Alone** | – | **190** | – |
| **We Give Thanks** | – | **192** | – |
| We have come to a throne | 311 | – | 7 |
| **We Rejoice in the Grace of God** | – | **194** | – |
| We resolve to know nothing else | – | 108 | 9 |
| **We See Your Holiness** | – | **196** | – |
| We share in the triumph | – | 180 | – |
| **We Sing Your Mercies** | – | **198** | **2,10** |
| **We Trust in God** | – | **200** | – |
| **We're Thirsting for You** | – | **202** | – |
| **We've Been Chosen** | – | **204** | – |
| **What a Glorious Mystery** | – | **206** | **9** |
| **What a Hope** | – | **208** | – |
| What a hope you've treasured up | 157 | – | 2 |
| What drew you to me | 115 | – | 2 |
| What I once called gain | – | 120 | 5 |
| **What Love Is This?** | – | **210** | – |
| What wisdom once devised | – | 134 | 7,12 |
| **What You Began** | – | **213** | **5** |
| When I look all around me | 245 | – | 3 |
| When I look upon the cross | – | 78 | 12 |
| When I see the stars in heaven | 228 | – | 14 |
| When I'm all alone | – | 113 | 13 |
| When I'm weak | – | 300 | 6 |
| When the cares of life come | – | 81 | 1 |
| When this world is filled | 270 | – | 6 |
| Who am I to draw near you? | 6 | – | 1 |
| Who can comprehend | – | 206 | 9 |
| Who is holding the sands of time? | 17 | – | 2 |
| **Who Is Like Our God** | – | **216** | **8** |
| **Who Is Like You?** | – | **219** | **13** |
| **Wonder on Wonder** | – | **221** | – |
| **Wonderful Savior** | – | **223** | **12** |
| You alone are the Almighty God | 211 | – | – |
| **You Are Always with Me** | – | **225** | **13** |
| You are beautiful | 252 | – | 10 |
| You are compassionate | 199 | – | – |
| **You Are Faithful** | – | **227** | – |
| **You Are Gentle** | – | **229** | – |

| SONG TITLE | VOL 1 | VOL 2 | CD |
|---|---|---|---|
| **You Are Greater** | – | **231** | – |
| *You are high above all things* | – | 292 | 8 |
| *You are high and lifted up* | – | 248 | – |
| **You Are Lord** | – | **234** | 10 |
| **You Are My Everything** | – | **236** | 7 |
| **You Are My First Love** | – | **239** | – |
| **You Are My God** | – | **241** | – |
| *You are the mighty warrior* | 164 | – | 8 |
| **You Are the One** | – | **242** | 1 |
| *You are the one and only God* | – | 151 | 3 |
| *You are the One who spoke* | 48 | – | 9 |
| *You are the perfect* | 237 | – | 12 |
| **You Are the Way** | – | **244** | 14 |
| **You Called Us Friends** | – | **248** | – |
| *You came to seek and to save* | – | 24 | – |
| *You did not wait for me* | 272 | – | – |
| *You gave your promise* | 190 | – | – |
| *You gently pursued me* | – | 323 | – |
| *You have ascended* | – | 294 | – |
| *You have become for us wisdom* | 28 | – | – |
| **You Have Been Given** | – | **251** | – |
| **You Have Been My Confidence** | – | **253** | – |
| **You Have Captured Me** | – | **255** | 7 |
| **You Have Exalted** | – | **257** | 5 |
| **You Have the Power** | – | **260** | – |
| **You Heavens Adore Him** | – | **264** | 11 |
| *You knew us each by name* | – | 285 | – |
| *You know everything about me* | – | 225 | 13 |
| **You Left Your Glory** | – | **270** | – |
| **You Sat Down** | – | **272** | – |
| *You say, "Come, you weary"* | 90 | – | 3 |
| *You were beaten with lashes* | 204 | – | – |
| *You were God all yesterday* | 133 | – | 13 |
| *You were not ashamed to be* | – | 185 | 9 |
| **You'll Never Leave Me** | – | **273** | – |
| **Your Beauty and Your Majesty** | – | **277** | 9 |
| *Your faithfulness and love* | 30 | – | 4 |
| *Your glory is what I am longing for* | 26 | – | 5 |
| *Your goodness found us* | 287 | – | 14 |
| **Your Great Name We Praise** | – | **280** | 11 |
| **Your Great Renown** | – | **283** | 7 |
| **Your Great Salvation** | – | **285** | – |
| **Your Hand Upon Me** | – | **288** | 8 |
| **Your Holiness Is Beautiful** | – | **290** | 5 |
| **Your Holy Majesty** | – | **292** | 8 |
| **Your Kingdom Is Glorious** | – | **294** | – |
| **Your Love** | – | **296** | 13 |
| **Your Love for Me** | – | **298** | 4 |
| **Your Love Is Higher** | – | **300** | 6 |
| **Your Love Stands Firm** | – | **303** | 3 |
| **Your Mercy and Kindness** | – | **306** | 8 |
| **Your Own Love** | – | **308** | – |
| **Your Praise Will Never Cease** | – | **310** | 7 |
| **Your Redeeming Love** | – | **312** | 7 |
| **Your Sovereign Grace** | – | **315** | 4 |
| **Your Word, O Lord** | – | **318** | – |
| *You're not ashamed* | – | 178 | – |
| **You're So Good to Me** | – | **321** | 5,10 |
| *You're the One who flung the stars* | – | 242 | 1 |
| **You've Captured My Heart** | – | **323** | – |
| *You've given me so much* | – | 321 | 5,10 |

**CD KEY**

1 *Love Beyond Degree* (Come & Worship 1)
2 *All for You* (Come & Worship 2)
3 *Depth of Mercy* (Come & Worship 3)
4 *Glory of the Ages* (Come & Worship 4)
5 *Lift a Shout* (Come & Worship 5)
6 *Everlasting* (Come & Worship 6)
7 *King of Grace* (Come & Worship 7)
8 *No Greater Love* (Come & Worship 8)
9 *All We Long to See* (Come & Worship 9)
10 *I Stand in Awe*
11 *Upward: The Bob Kauflin Hymns Project*
12 *Songs for the Cross Centered Life*
13 *Awesome God*
14 *Worship God Live*

The songs on these CDs may also be purchased as individual downloads in MP3 format.

Just visit The Songbox in the Music section at www.SovereignGraceStore.com. There you can download songs from our back catalog, as well as recently released Songbox Singles. God-glorifying, MP3 format, and 99 cents each. What's not to like?

# SCRIPTURE INDEX

# MORE WORSHIP RESOURCES FROM SOVEREIGN GRACE

Sovereign Grace Ministries produces a number of resources designed to help churches make music—as the Foreword to this songbook puts it—"for the praise of the triune God whose glory knows no end." Here are just a few of those resources.

### THE SONGBOX

One at a time or by the box-full. We're regularly adding new songs to the Songbox—from songs on current recordings to newly released Songbox Singles. Open the Box at **www.SovereignGraceStore.com**

### WORSHIP MATTERS

Our director of worship development, Bob Kauflin, writes a blog called Worship Matters. While Worship Matters is intended primarily to serve those who lead corporate praise (such as pastors, musicians, and small-group leaders), anyone who wants to use music and words to magnify God's glory in Christ should find something helpful here. **www.worshipmatters.com**

### WORSHIPGOD CONFERENCE

This bi-annual conference exists to equip the entire church—with specific emphasis on those who lead corporate praise—in the principles and practices of God-honoring worship. General sessions on a specific theological theme are augmented by practical seminars for vocalists, musicians, audio technicians, and others. **www.SovereignGraceMinistries.org/conferences**

**We also produce CDs of Christ-centered, cross-centered worship music. Here are four of our most recent.**

### UPWARD: THE BOB KAUFLIN HYMNS PROJECT

This project emerges from a conviction that hymns still speak with power. A pastor, worship leader, and songwriter, Bob selected, adapted, and arranged these twelve songs—some of them familiar, some new, and some newly revised. Each one directs our gaze upward to our magnificent God and Savior.

### SONGS FOR THE CROSS CENTERED LIFE

This CD was inspired by a little orange book called *The Cross Centered Life*, by C.J. Mahaney. The book was written to help remind our forgetful souls of the one glorious truth that should be the very core of our existence: the gospel. Like the book, the songs on this CD are intended to remind us of Christ and him crucified—and to lead us to worship him.

### AWESOME GOD

*Awesome God* is our first Sovereign Grace Kids release. Geared to ages 7 and up, the songs celebrate various attributes of God. Grownups like the CD, too, for it combines God-centered lyrics with top-quality musicianship and arrangements. *Awesome God* is a great resource for families, or for the children's ministry in your church.

### WORSHIP GOD LIVE

The most recent of several live recordings from Sovereign Grace, this 14-song CD, recorded over two nights at Covenant Life Church in Gaithersburg, Maryland, features worship leaders Bob Kauflin and Pat Sczebel. *Worship God Live* is the only CD on this page with songs too new to appear in this two-volume songbook, but you can download sheet music for those songs (and many others) from our website.

**www.SovereignGraceStore.com**